CITY AND URBAN FRINGE

CITY AND URBAN FRINGE
(A Case Study of Bareilly)

H. LAL

I.C.S.S.R Consultant
Prof. S.L. Kayastha

CONCEPT PUBLISHING COMPANY, NEW DELHI

ISBN: 81-7022-190-0

Reprinted 2007
First Published 1987

Published and Printed by
Ashok Kumar Mittal
Concept Publishing Company
A/15-16, Commercial Block, Mohan Garden
New Delhi-110 059 (INDIA)
Phones : 25351460, 25351794 *Fax* : 091-11-25357103
Email : publishing@conceptpub.com

Preface

In the past much work in urban geography has been strongly influenced by the idea of a unicentered city, with various urban land uses and their associated human activities being assessed in terms of distance from the city centre. Current research is tending to move away from this standpoint, since increasingly the expansion of many cities is taking place at a considerable distance from the city centre and often with much less relation to conditions there than was observable in earlier decades. Of course, the growth and decline of individual landuses and human activities occur in all parts of the city but, in absolute terms, change is particularly concentrated in and around the city centre and on the outer periphery of the built-up area (Johnson, 1970).

Changes in land use and population at or close to the city centre have been long-standing geographical features, stimulated by the high value of land and the resulting need for constant readjustments in buildings and landuses, as associated human activities attempt to extract the maximum benefit out of expensive central locations. It can be argued, however, that over the years the process of geographical change in the inner parts of cities has received more than its fair share of attention, possibly because change here is more easily noticed, and because the redevelopment of residential areas close to the centre poses particularly difficult social problems.

But changes on the edge of the city, although less concentrated and involving less dramatic social issues, are of much greater total importance, since a larger area of land is involved and the day-to-day lives of more people are likely to be affected. In addition many geographical changes at the urban periphery are associated with the transfer of land from rural to urban purposes, which may be a more fundamental alteration than many other landuse changes which take place in urban areas. The interaction between rural and urban is, thus, at its maximum at the outer edge of the continuously built-up area since here is located the undeveloped space into which a town or city expands by circumferential or radial growth. This is the urban fringe which has been a neglected field of research both by urban geographers as well as regional planners.

The accelerating expansion of Indian cities and towns during recent decades is making increasingly serious inroads into formerly rural territories and confusion is usually a major characteristic of the overmoving boundary between the two. Sound planning based on accurate detailed knowledge of conditions is therefore an urgent requirement if unnecessary hardship, costly mistakes and future regrets are to be avoided. It is with this objective that this work is concerned.

The present study is an attempt to analyse the growth and development of Bareilly city for understanding and interpretation of some of its features with a view to applying the geographer's method of survey and analysis to planning for its orderly growth in future. Bareilly, a regional headquarter situated on the left bank of the Ramganga in the Rohilkhand Plain, has been taken as a case study which is growing rapidly with the establishment of important industries and expansion of urban functions near its periphery. As a result a zone of mixed landuse has been evolved and has created problems to the concerned authorities. Thus, after delineating the urban fringe and assessing the impact of the city on surrounding villages as well as analysing the major problems, a comprehensive plan for the future development of the city has been provided.

The systematic and comprehensive account of Bareilly and its urban fringe is presented in seven chapters dealing with different aspects as follows. The study commences with the discussion of the geographical background that has determined the location of the urban centre on the present site. Chapter I is devoted to the study of the evolution of the townscape, its origin and growth and its morphological characteristics. Chapter II raises the most controversial issues of the determination of the urban fringe. Here an attempt has been made to delimit the urban fringe of Bareilly after examining a number of indices applied for the purpose. Chapter III deals with the demographic characteristics of

vii Preface

the city as well as its fringe. Some latest statistical techniques, like gradient analysis and residual mapping, have been used to analyse the spatial distribution of population in the area. Chapter IV seeks to explain the functional landuse in the city while next chapter is devoted to analyse the settlement and landuse pattern in the fringe. Special attention has been paid in this chapter to bring into light the various factors responsible for the distribution and changing pattern of landuse in the peripheral region. The appraisal of different amenities and services available in both the city and the fringe is the subject matter of Chapter VI. Finally the study concludes with an assessment of the problems, the city and its fringe is confronted with. From the view point of planning, the potentiality of different sectors of the fringe have been determined, and important suggestions for landuse zoning and landuse planning have been made.

The whole study is based on the interpretation of about sixty maps and diagrams based on the materials collected from different sources during the course of extensive field work.

HIRA LAL

Reader,
Department of Geography,
University of Gorakhpur,
GORAKHPUR-273009

Acknowledgement

I am extremely grateful to Prof. U. Singh, Retired Prof. and Head of the Department of Geography, University of Gorakhpur for his constructive criticism and helpful suggestions throughout the course of my work. Thanks are also due to Sri Satya Prakash, Co-planner, Bareilly Survey Division and various officials of the Municipal Corporation for their help in data collection.

I owe much to Dr. J. Singh, Professor and Head for extending the departmental help, and Mr. Chandrabhan for redrawing some maps of the book. I express my deep gratefulness to Prof. R.L. Singh, Prof. S.L. Kayastha, Prof. R. Ramchandran and Dr. V.K. Shrivastava from whom I received many valuable suggestions.

Financial assistance provided by Indian Council of Social Science Research (ICSSR) New Delhi, towards publication of this book is gratefully acknowledged. The entire responsibility for the views expressed as also for any error of analysis or facts which may appear is, of course, solely that of the author.

My thanks are due to Sri Naurang Rai of the Concept Publishing Company for publishing the book within a very short span of time.

The author's family, wife Smt. Madhuri and children, Nimisha, Manisha, Vivek and Shilpi, also deserve special thanks for their moral support, forbearance and encouragement which enabled the author to complete this book in a short time.

Abhigyan, Mohaddipur, H. LAL
Gorakhpur - 273008

Contents

List of Figures

List of Tables

ONE

Evolution of Bareilly

Bareilly (28°22' N and and 79° 24' E) properly spelled Bareli and commonly known as Bans Bareli to distinguish it from Rae-Bareli in Awadh, is the divisional headquarters of Rohilkhand. Situated almost in the heart of the district it lies 255 km north-west of Lucknow, the state capital and about 252 km east of Delhi on the Lucknow-Delhi section of the Northern Railway which skirts the city in the west. It enjoys a central position in the Upper Ganga Plain North and is the second largest city after Lucknow (Fig.1.1).

SITE

Bareilly is situated on the eastern high bank of the Ramganga, a northern tributary of the Ganga. The city lies in the Ramganga basin in between Deorania in the west and Nakatia in the east, both being the tributaries of the Ramganga. The Ramganga has been shifting its course towards west leaving its old beds in the east. It has two channels several kilometers apart and the river keeps shifting from one to the another and cutting into the land in between. Within last 50 years it has shifted about 2-3 km west leaving the eastern old beds inundated and marshy during rains.

The main Urban Settlement extends in west-east direction in a riverine plain stretching between 164.5 m (540') in the west to (172 m 565') in the central and 167.5 m (550') in the east (Fig.1.2) with an average elevations of 167.5 metres (550') above the sea level. From the centre (172 m 565') the region slopes to different direction but more towards the west.

The natural drainage of the area has been highly affected by the railway lines running on embankments. The Northern railway skirting the town from south west runs on high old bank of the Ramganga. The metre gauge railway line coming from north joins the city Railway station skirting the city from the north-west. These railway lines acting as cultural divides, have restricted the natural flow of water. In the consequence the part of the Ramganga basin on which the town stands have bad drainage system and a greater part of the city is often inundated during rains.

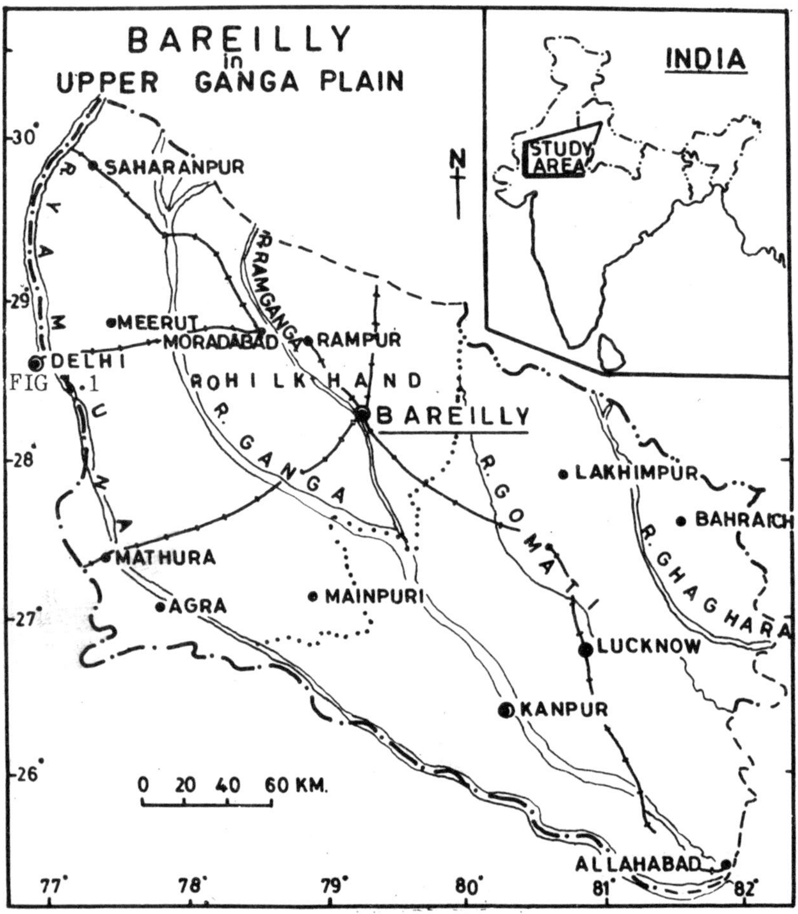

FIG. 1.1

CLIMATIC CHARACTERISTICS

Bareilly is situated in the sub-tropical interior part of the Ganga Plain. Its climate is Sub-Himalayan in character and being largely influenced by the proximity of the hills and the 'tarai' in the north. The city is directly affected by the heavier storms in the hills, with the result that rainy season commences a few days earlier and terminates somewhat later than in the districts to the south while the cold weather is of longer duration.

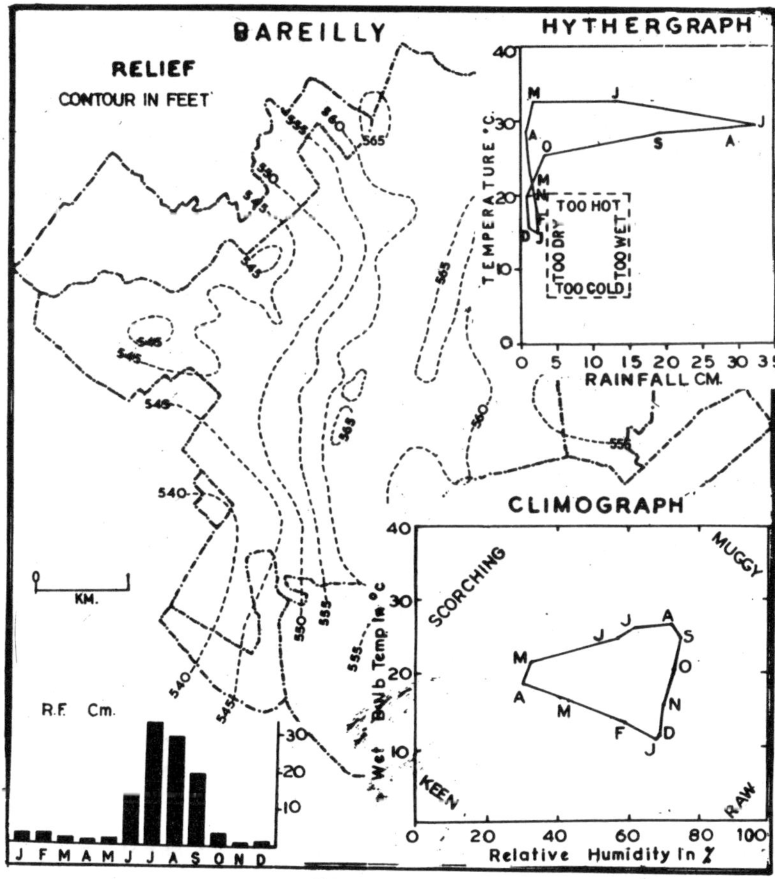

FIG. 1.2

The influence of the 'tarai' is marked with the relative dampness of the climate and other characteristics are moderate heat in summer and immunity from violent hot winds. The temperature is lowered from time to time by thunderstorms in May, sometimes accompanied by rains.

Before the actual arrival of the monsoon the winds shift

from the west to south and with the first fall of rain, the temperature drops sharply. During this season the mornings are pleasant but the evenings are usually oppressive and the climate of Bareilly at this season becomes far less enjoyable than that of the drier districts. Towards the end of the rains it is decidedly unhealthy.

The temperature begins to fall from the end of the september and continues till the end of February in winter season. The winter season experiences a considerable intensity of frost.

TEMPERATURE

From about the middle of November temperature decreases rapidly and in January, the coldest month, the mean daily minimum and maximum temperature drops to 8.1° c and 21.6° c respectively. In association with the cold waves in the wake of western disturbances passing eastward, the minimum temperature sometimes may go down to even the freezing point when frosts often occur.

After February temperature begins to rise rapidly. May and early June constitute the hottest period of the year. In May, the mean daily minimum and maximum temperature marked 39.7° c and 25.2° c respectively. The hot dry westerly wind (loo) make the heat more intense but rarely blow after sunset. Thunder storms usually follow dust-storm in this period and bring some relief from the heat. By mid June with the advancement of the S.W. Monsoon, day temperature drops appreciably but nights continue to be warm as in the summer.

The increased humidity during rainy season causes general oppressiveness. In October nights become cool although day temperatures continue to be as high as in the monsoon season.

The highest maximum temperature recorded at Bareilly was 46.7° c on May 29, 1884, and the lowest minimum temperature was 0.0° c on Feb. 2,1905.

RAINFALL

The normal annual rainfall in the area is 1102 mm and the average number of rainydays is 46. The rainfall generally increases from the south-west towards the northeast of the district as it is marked 982.1mm at Aonla (S.W.corner) to 1259.7 mm at Baheri (in North). About 87 percent of the annual rainfall is recorded during the monsoon season, while July being the month with the maximum rainfall.(Fig.1.2).

WINDS

Winds are generally light and calm in the mornings. Westerlies and north-westerlies are more common from October to April. By May, the wind system is reversed and east and south-west winds predominate thereafter and continue during the rainy season.

SPECIAL WEATHER PHENOMENA

During the summer months the city experiences duststorms and thunder-storm with occasional squalls. In the monsoon months, the rain is often associated with thunderstorms which also occur in association with spells of inclement weather during the winter when fog is fairly common.

MICRO-CLIMATE

Most of the elements of the regional climate are modified slightly in the city area due to its settlement concentration. Pollution of atmosphere is the first effect of urban development. The solid, liquid and gaseous impurities emitted from the multiplicity of industrial and domestic chimneys and automobiles etc. are important factors in modifying the micro-climate of the city. The degree of pollution and its effect on climate may be marked more in the central core than the peripheral areas.

HUMAN COMFORT

The generalized climograph applied to Bareilly (Fig.1.2) shows that the weather conditions of the city are not uncomfortable for the greater parts of the year.

ORIGIN AND GROWTH OF BAREILLY

ORIGIN

Bareilly was not an important settlement before the establishment of Mughal empire. During this period the foundation of the present town was laid by Raja Jagat Singh Katehriya, the governor of the region. It is said that about the year 1500. A.D. Jagat Singh founded a village called Jagatpur (now a muhalla in the eastern margin of the old city), and in 1537 his sons Bans Deo and Barel Deo founded the township near Jagatpur which became later popular as Bans Bareili after the names of two brothers.

The another story about the origin of the town goes that Jagat Singh was a Barhela Rajput and had two sons Bans Deo and Nagdeo, of whom the former built the fort called Bans Bareili in 1550, while the latter founded part of the new city. Later on, the city is said to derive its name Bans Bareilly to distinguish it from another city, Rae Bareli in Awadh. It is further said that the neighbouring area was full of bamboo trees (Bans tree) and so it was added to the name of the city as a prefix.

THE EARLIER TOWNSCAPE

A small town gradually developed around the fort and became the headquarters of a pargana in 1596. During the regime of Akbar, Mirzai Masjid and Mirzai Bagh were built. During Shahjahan period this town became the capital of Katehr and the new governor Raja Makrand Rai Khatri developed a new city about 2 km. west of the old site in 1657. He built a new fort alongwith the tomb of Shahdana and the Jami Masjid on the north. The foundations of Makrandpur, Alamgiriganj, Malukpur, Kunwarpur and Biharipur are also ascribed either to him or his brothers.

After the death of Aurangzeb in 1707 Rohillas consolidated their positions in this area and there after the region became known as Rohilkhand (Hamilton.1787). The town was occupied by Ali Mohammad in 1740. During his regime the headquarter of the area was shifted to Aonla and Bareilly sank into insignificance. It was again made a political headquarters in 1774 and since then a number of mohallas, as Katra Chandkhan, Bajaria Sandalkhan, Zulfiquarganj and Garhi Manrai were added. Later on, the town together with the region, fell into the hands of the Nawab of Awadh after the war of Rohilla in 1774.

During the time of East India company the town and the area was ceded to the company and Bareilly became the headquarters of district and since then a number of administrative and commercial activities took place (Fig.1.3). further a number of new shopping zones and residential areas were added to the townscape of old Bareilly. Roads were constructed to link the city with Nainital, Pilibhit, Moradabad and Furrukhabad etc. which further facilitated the develop-

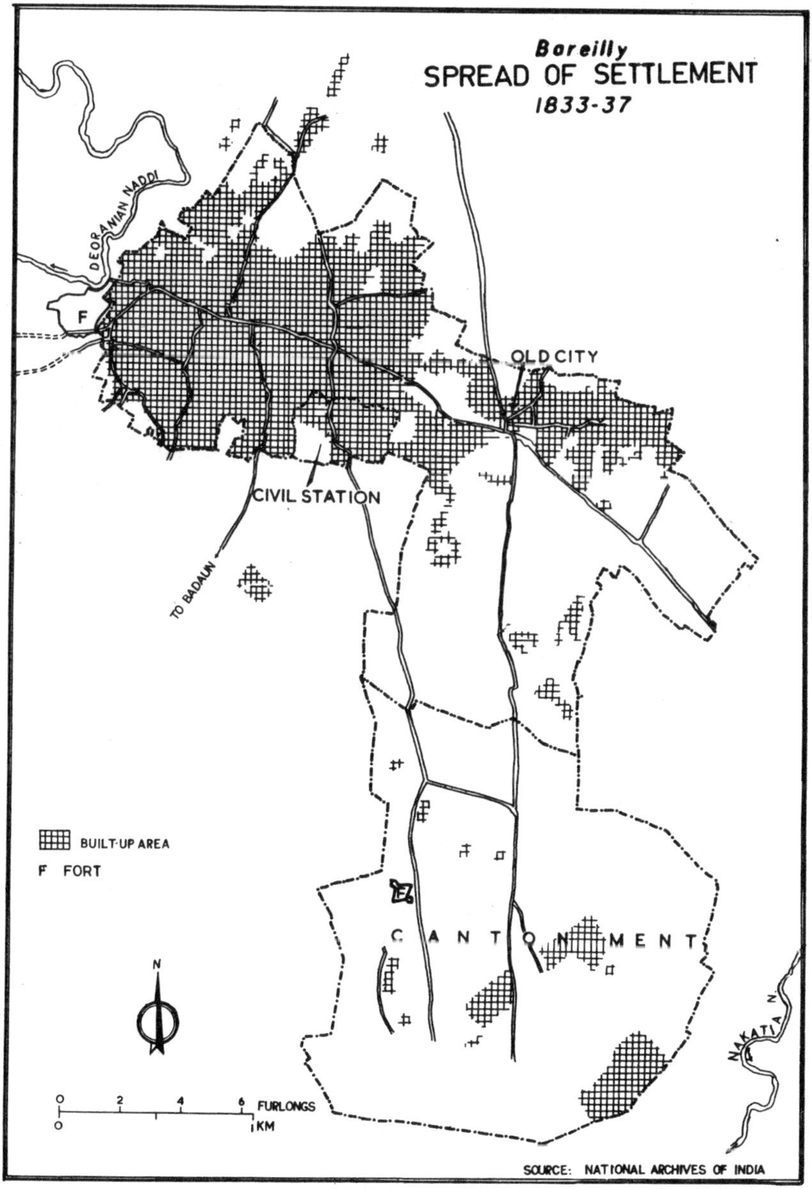

Bareilly
SPREAD OF SETTLEMENT
1833-37
DEORANIAN NADDI
F
OLD CITY
CIVIL STATION
TO BADAUN
BUILT-UP AREA
F FORT
CANTONMENT
N
NAKATIA N.
0 2 4 6 FURLONGS
0 1 KM
SOURCE: NATIONAL ARCHIVES OF INDIA

FIG. 1.3

ment of trade and commerce at this centre. During the same period another important aspect of cultural landscape came into being with the establishment of Bareilly Cantonment in 1811 in the southern suburb of the town bounded in the east by the Nakatia river. This area contained by this time more public buildings than any other part of the city (Conybeare-1879).

During the first war of independence of 1857 Khan Bahadurkhan proclaimed himself as the governor of this place and Bareilly remained independent of the rule of the East India company for sometimes till the town was recaptured by the British army on 5 May 1858. The Municipal Board of Bareilly was constructed in 1858.

During the British Rule, the city became an important railway junction with the construction of Oudh and Rohilkhand Kumaun Railways in 1873. A metre gauge railway with Lucknow-Bareilly-Delhi Broadgauge railway was constructed in 1884.

Close of the nineteenth century witnessed some major addition to the townscape with the establishment of a number of social and cultural elements. In 1870 the American presbyterian Mission started two Anglo Vernacular schools in the city and two such schools by Arya Samaj at Beharipur and Bhoor in 1882. Several institutions including English Memorial school were founded in different parts of the town during this period.

Central Jail Hospital at Izatnagar in 1837, the Clara Swain Hospital in 1875, the Dufferin Hospital in 1889 and State Hospital in 1891 were added to provide medical facilities to the city and its environs. Further provision of telegraph and Bank services stimulated the smooth running of the business and commerce in the city.

Developed in between the city and Cantonment, the Civil Lines laid out by Britishers in the latter part of the nineteenth Century was another land mark in the extension of the townscape. The civil lines were meant exclusively for civil officers residences. The district courts, the police lines and magistrate lockup etc. were situated in the southern area near railway station. The district Jail in the west and officials bungalows including circuit house were located in this north-east part of the Civil Lines. The eastern part was developed from north to south with Lunatic Hospital (Mental hospital building), Carpentry school and company Bagh in a line (Fig.1.4).

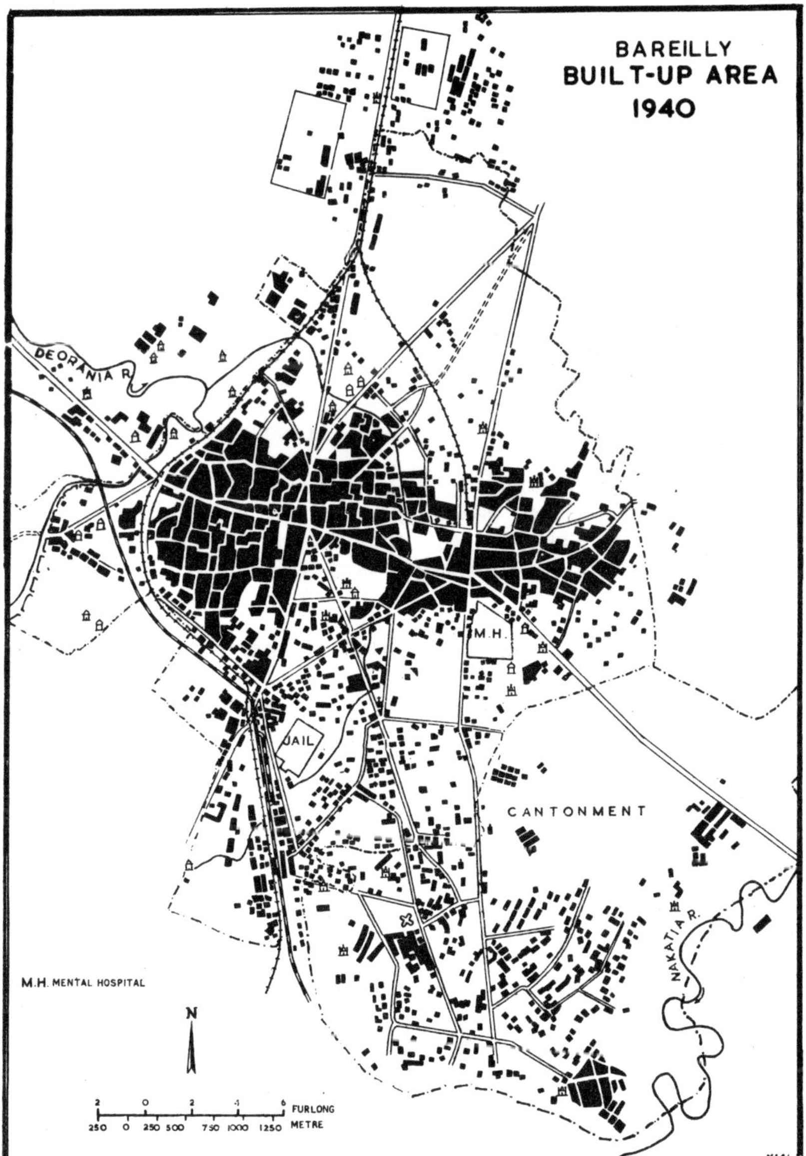

FIG. 1.4

THE CITY PROPER

By this time the main city had extended more towards west than the east. It then consisted of two zones.

(i)The old city area to the east of Pilibhit-Shahjahanpur Road with Golganj square. Its muslim majority area having greater percentage of open spaces, grave yards, old mosques and dilapidated houses.

(ii)The New city lies on either side of the main street from Golganj westwards. It was flanked on either side by a continuous line of neat masonry shops with two storied buildings. To the south of the main street lie the mohallas of Shahmatganj, Kalibari, Bansmandi etc. and they developed as business-cum-residential areas. The municipal office was also constructed here in a large triangular enclosure with a well maintained garden as its annexe in the south. To the north different residential areas were developed. The most densely inhabited block of city at this time was in between the Nainital Road and the railway lines (Fig.1.4).

Beyond the railway line in the west, important settlements were suburb of Salehnagar including Hussainbagh and the garden of Champat Rai. The Tomb of Hafiz Rahmat Khan, erected in 1834, was an important cultural land-scape of that area.

GROWTH OF PRESENT TOWNSCAPE PRIOR TO 1947

Accelerated development of trade and commerce, transport, industries and other socio-economic activities in the city occurred in the beginning of the twentieth century(Azad-1970). A number of industrial concerns on modern lines such as the National Brewery Co., a match factory, an ice factory and a steam flour mill etc. followed after the construction of the Rohilkhand and Kumaun railways in the first decade of the present century . The Central Wood Working Institute for carrying research in the artificial seasoning of timber for railway requirements, was also established during this period.

The Indian Turpentine & Rosin Co. (1924) and the Western Indian Match Co. (WIMCO,1938) were established at Clutterbuckganj about 8km. west of the city. The Indian Wood Products Ltd. started in 1919 at Izatnagar, to extract catechu on the large scale.H.R.Sugar factory was built in 1932 in Nekpur, the southern outer part of the city on

Budaun Road adding much to the townscape (Fig.1.4).

In the thirties and early forties, Bareilly emerged as an important trade centre. Several branches of banks, commercial concerns and many educational institutions were opened in different parts of the town.

GROWTH AFTER INDEPENDENCE

After independence, a number of new industrial concerns were added to the already existing factories. Clutter Buckganj emerged as an important industrial node and Izatnagar developed as an important industrial-cum-transport centre in the vicinity of the city which ultimately accelerated the pace of economic and physical growth of the city. Further, the establishment of the Khandsari, furniture, engineering, oil and ice industries located in Naibasti and shahmatganj provided a solid base for the growth of the town. As a result Bareilly became the main trade centre of the district. The Shahmatganj and Quilla market developed as the biggest mandis of the region.

Consequently new government buildings came into existence in different parts of the city. The Civil Lines expanded towards its north-east and a new public-cum-residential colony, known as Rampur garden was developed in between old city and Cantonment area. Most of the government offices are located either in the Civil Lines or in Rampur garden.

Further, certain important community facilities and amenities were added to the townscape. The waterworks came into existence in 1957 and the wider area of town was electrified in 1960. Several new educational institutions were established including I.T.I. and polytechnic. As a result considerable migration took place from the adjoining country-side causing establishment of new residential colonies in the suburban areas of the city. The railway colonies of Shahdana, Izatnagar, Chaupala and Cantonment were built by the Railway departments. The land and rental values sprang up in the older part due to which the development of new colonies like Prem Nagar, Subashnagar etc. took place in the outer zones. In other words, greater development of city took place after the Independence in the spheres of industry,commerce, social and economic activities, thus placing Bareilly among the important cities of U.P. (Fig.1.5).

BAREILLY
BUILT-UP AREA
1971
TO N. TAL
TO PILIBHIT
TO RAMPUR
TO SHAHJAHANPUR
CANTONMENT
TO BADAUN
2 0 2 4 6 FURLONG
250 0 250 500 750 1000 1250 METRE

FIG. 1.5

CHARACTERISTICS OF EXISTING TOWNSCAPE

The morphology of this city is characterised by unplanned old Indian town with narrow lanes, old types of clustured houses and crowded shops. The residential areas of the inner part of the town still present a most unsatisfactory look. The slums and blighted areas occur at intervals in the different parts of the city. In contrast to the old city, there have developed a planned, better class residential colony in the south.

During sixties and seventies, some important shopping centres, like Subash market, Chaupala , Punjabi and Kishore markets have come-up in the newly developed residential areas along Kutubkhana-Junction road. Pantmarket has recently been added to the townscape as a most fashionable shopping enclave near Yakubkhan crossing. But the heart of the city still beats in the central business district lying in the centre.

The Civil Lines between the city and the cantonment have been developed in a planned way. Of several important institutions located in this part mention may be made of Bareilly College, Mental Hospital, Central Woodwork Institute and the Court.

Gandhi Park and Jubilee Park are the important recreational centres situated in the civil lines. Rampur Garden colony in south, Refugee colony and Model town in the north have further added a planned dimension to the city structure.

The Cantonment in the southern part is a restricted area and less has been added to this part since long. Recently the expansion of a central zone of Indian Air force in the extreme north, though far away from the city limit, have resulted in the addition of a number of building in the area.

In the north within municipal limit there is a stretch of openland of about 3 km^2 beyond which lies Izatnagar including a railway station, N.E.R.Workshop, Hospital, and its staff quarters, Veterinary Research Institute(I.V.R.I), central and U.P. Govt. irrigation workshop etc. within it. All these have changed the landuse of this area considerably.

EXPANSION OF BUILT-UP AREA

By 1837 the built-up area had expanded considerably around the older settlements. Thereafter until 1911, the major developments took place in the Civil Lines and the city proper. Between 1911 to 1940, the built-up area of the city extended towards the west and the north-east (Fig.1.4). The post Independence years marked the filling-up of the vacant areas within the older part of the city and the expansion of the built-up area on south-west and the areas beyond shahdana railway line in the north especially west of Pilibhit Road (Fig.1.5).

THE PROCESS OF GROWTH

Three traditional theories relating to the process of city growth are partly applicable to Bareilly. The city depicted the concentric zone form (elongated shape) in the early stage of its development process, being principal centre of wholesaling and retailing upto the end of the nineteenth century (Fig.1.6A). The segregational trend in the growth pattern became more prominent in the beginning of the 20th century with increase in urban complexes. The first sector developed along Nainital road while second towards west on Rampur road.

Presently C.B.Ganj, Izatnagar and I.V.R.I have their impact as an important nuclei for the further growth of the city.

GEOGRAPHICAL ZONES

Differences in the pattern of settlements, types of houses, social and economic structures and the types of land use have helped to divide the city in four geographical zones: the inner zone, the middle zone, the outer zone and the suburban zone (Fig.1.6B).

THE INNER ZONE

This zone corresponds with the old Rohilla city. It includes whole of the central part of the city stretching from Shahmatganj to Quilla, characterised by narrow zig-zag lanes and streets, housing multistoreyed buildings. It is highly built and congested part of the city. The western subzone of this core region is the trade and commercial zone. The eastern zone is highly congested with old residential houses, especially of old city's blighted area.

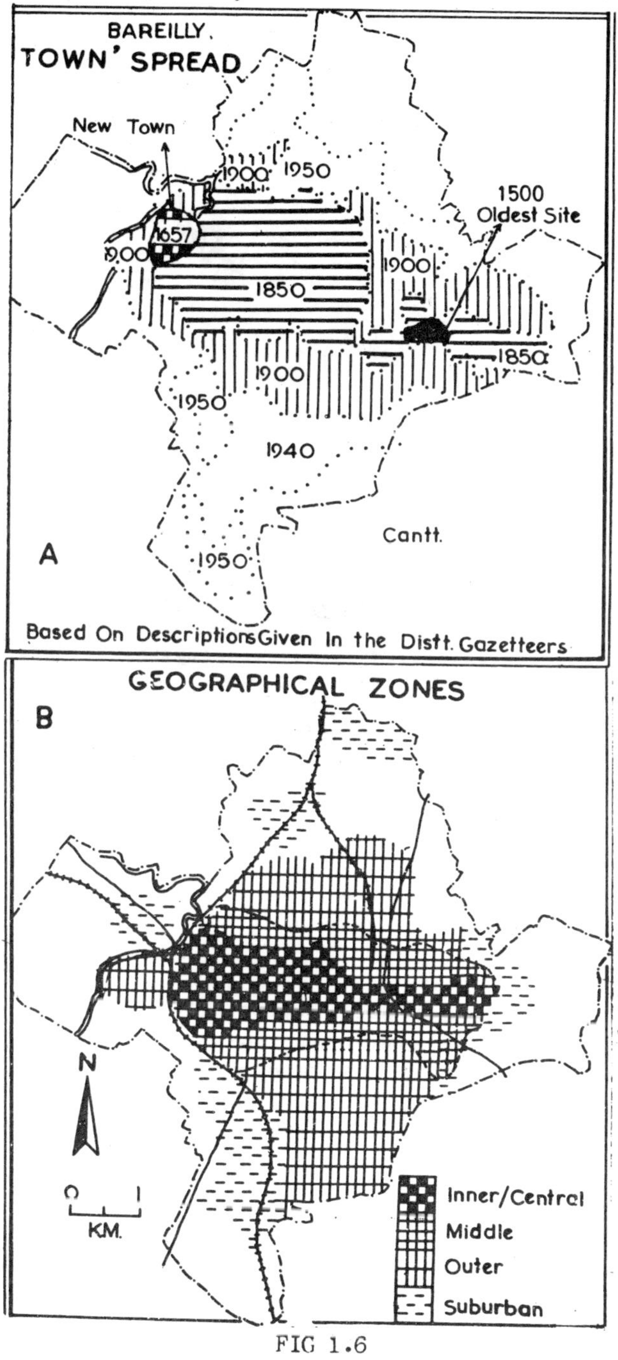
BAREILLY.
TOWN' SPREAD
New Town
1900
1950
1500
Oldest Site
1657
1900
1900
1850
1850
1900
1950
1940
Cantt.
A
1950
Based On Descriptions Given In the Distt. Gazetteers
GEOGRAPHICAL ZONES
B
N
0
KM.
Inner/Central
Middle
Outer
Suburban

FIG 1.6

FIG 1.7

THE MIDDLE ZONE

Extending in east-west direction on both sides of the fully built-up inner zone lies the middle zone which was erected mainly during the late nineteenth century. The north-eastern parts of this zone are mixed with industrial establishments. Its southern part is comparatively open.

THE OUTER ZONE

This includes large peripneral lands to the north and south of the above zones. Its settlements are scattered, residential density is low and its thoroughfares are of minor importance to business. Although development started in the early 1930's, most of it took place after 1947. The southern zone comprises the Civil Lines which represents a different aspect of the townscape having distinct geographical characteristics in its street pattern, house types and functional character and also in its types of residential areas. The planned and newly developed high and middle class residential areas; administrative, educational and recreational sections with some old bustees of Baquarganj in west are the main features of this zone.

THE SUBURBAN ZONE

This zone is located peripherally to the north, east, south-west and west in the recently extended part of the municipality. The development here started slowly in the late 1960's. This zone presents the rural character as the residential areas are separated from one another by long distances and sometimes by agricultural fields. The villages of this zone are compact and are inhabited by low-class people. Madhinath, Nekpur and Newadajogian villages lack most of the civic amenities and represent dilapidated dingy conditions, especially in rainy season.

ADMINISTRATIVE UNITS

From an administrative point of view the entire corporation area (25.36Sq.km.) has been divided into 16 wards (Fig.1.7). There are 520 enumerators blocks in 114 mohallas. Recently 10 villages have partly been included in the municipal limit.

SELECTED REFERENCES

1. Azad, P.C. (1970) Bareilly District in **District Board Report**, pp.3-17.
2. Conybeare, H.C.(1879) **Statistical Description and Historical Account of the N.W.Provinces of India**, Vol. V. Rohilkhand Division, Allahabad.
3. Hamilton,C.(1787) **An Historical Relation of the Origin, Progress and Final Dissolution of the Rohilla Afghans in the new provinces of Hindustan** pp.111-112.
4. Joshi, E.B. (1968) U.P. **District Gazetteers: Bareilly**, Allahabad.
5. Sharma, S.L. (1965) **Zila Bareilly Ka Parichaya**, Jawahar Prakashan, Budaun.
6. Singh, U.et.al. (1971) 'Upper Ganga Plain, in R.L.Singh(Ed.) **India: A Regional Geography** N.G.S.I.Varanasi.
7. Spate,O.H.K. (1957) **India and Pakistan**, IInd Ed.

TWO

Delimitation of the Urban Fringe

An important development in urban settlement during the past few decades has been the rapid expansion of population and built-up area into the unincorporated suburb and in areas surrounding our large towns and cities. This recent finger-like trend of development at the town margins has been made possible by the mechanised transportation and the extension of the public utility services such as electricity, water and sewage, etc. beyond the city's limit. The process of accretion which takes place outside the city has generated a zone of transition between the rural and urban landscape, properly known as the rural-urban fringe. In other words, the centrifugal forces which impel functions to migrate from the central zone of a city towards its periphery, create an amorphous territory around the cities, often called the rural-urban fringe. This is a new phenomenon in the urban land-scape of the developing countries of the world in general and of India in particular.

The emergence of the fringe zone with its complex problems of adjustment between rural and urban ways of life, has assumed great topical importance and has drawn the attention of planners and social scientists. Yet the study of the urban fringe has been a neglected area of urban research. Even in the developed countries a few studies have been undertaken in this regard though this developmental phase of urban morphology was experienced there in the very beginning of the present century. Fringe studies have not received much attention among Indians either from geographers or from scholars in any of the other disciplines. Hence, we have one of the major gaps in geographical research in this area of urban studies. The purpose of this chapter is therefore to clarify the conceptual framework of the urban fringe and to delineate the fringe area of

Bareilly a growing class I city of North India (U.P.).

THE URBAN FRINGE : CONCEPTS

A study of the available literature reveals that most of the studies appeared during the period from the mid-1940s to the beginning of 1960s, in which attention was focussed mainly to the physical delimitation, identification and the defining features of the rural-urban fringe. The term urban fringe was introduced by Smith(1937)[1] to describe built-up area just outside the corporate limit of the city "though the word 'rurban' as synonymous to fringe was used by Gaplin[2] as early as in 1915 for 'rural' land in process of conversion to 'urban'. Smith's definition was mainly concerned with the demographic characteristics of the area, therefore, it presented a general rather than a specific conceptualization of the fringe. Further, Salter (1940)[3] defined the fringe as a mixture of landuses that are related to farming and urban interest....' In his excellent study "The Rural Urban Fringe" Wehrwein (1942)[4] has called it an "institutional desert" because of the uncontrolled location there of unpleasant and noxious establishments such as slaughter-houses, junkyards and wholesale oil storage, and of utilities such as sewage plants and cemeteries. In his opinion, fringe is the area of mixed landuses lying beyond those sections of the city that are customarily serviced by urban utilities and transport systems. Further, he describes it as an area of transition between well-recognised urban landuses and the area devoted to agriculture. Thus, Wehrwein is very clear that the fringe area can better be identified in terms of landuses than in any other way.

Andrews (1942)[5] contributed new thought to the fringe studies by attempting to differentiate the urban fringe from the rural-urban fringe. The urban fringe, as he puts it, is the active expanding sector of the compact economic city and the rural-urban fringe lies adjacent to the periphery of the urban fringe. The year 1942 bore a special significance for such studies as after Wehrwein and Andrews, Klow (1942)[6] and Alpake (1942)[7] were also to emerge on the scene. Alpake has defined the urban fringe as "that cultural development that takes place outside the boundaries of central cities and extends to the areas of predominantly agricultural activities.

After 1942, there has been a gradual but notable widening in the scope of fringe studies. Balk (1954)[8] added a new term, as he found the fringe an area of "rurbanization". Laying emphasis upon the accessibility as a sole factor in the development of the fringe, Walter Fiery (1946)[9] said "the rurban fringe is a marginal landuse area not because of its geographical location, its soil type or its topography, but rather because of its particular degree of accessibility (relative to that of other landuse) to some central transportation point". Rodehaver (1947)[10] in his study "Fringe settlement as a two directional movement" reiterates that new residents converge upon the fringe both from urban places and rural areas. While Dewey (1948)[11] marked that the movement of population into the rural-urban fringe was a movement of urban people. He further adds"... in the fringe area there is mingling of people of some of whom work in and are oriented towards agriculture while at the same time the remainder pursue urban occupations and an urban way of life". The end of the forties saw a well marked deviation from the traditional line of definition and division in rural-urban fringe studies as Aschman (1949)[12] and Blizzard and Anderson (1952)[13] confined to landuse and Martin (1953)[14] to patterns of population.

Duncan (1956)[15] used the term fringe to denote the non-suburban population of the territory in urbanised areas outside the central cities. His urbanised area contained three components-central city, suburb and urban fringe. The urban fringe is limited to the corporate limit of the city and often it is found outside the limit also. Kurtz and Eicher (1958)[16] attempted to differentiate between fringe and suburb. Golledge (1960)[17] used the term 'geographical no-man's land" for this contact zone between rural and urban landuses. Similarly, Russwurm (1960)[18] refers to this area as "frontier of discontinuity between the city and country, while Conzen (1960)[19] has recognised the fringe belt as significant determinants of the morphology of urban settlements. Defining its character, he identifies, the fringe belt itself as composed of two sections, the "proximal" or inner margin where development is closer and more continuous and the "destal" or outer margin where growth is more sporadic and the development more dispersed in character. Wissink (1962)[20] in an extensive survey of the fringe areas of American cities identifies "fringe" "suburbs", "pseudo-suburbs", "satellites" and "pseudo-satellites" and in landuse terms has called it an area of "great differentiation". Pastalan (1967)[21] giving an operational definition of the fringe has defined it as an area in transition where rural landuses are giving way to urban landuses. Seeing all these differentiations in the definition, Whitehand (1967)[22] called the fringe a "heterogeneous region". In his view, they are examples of regions that derive their unity not from homogeneity of forms but from certain factors that influenced their location.

Pryor (1968-69)[23] faced another aspect of the problem of definition when he noted and attempted to resolve the various areal differentiations of the urban fringe which have been proposed. In his view the rural-urban fringe may quantitatively be sub-divided into an "urban fringe" and a "rural fringe" on the basis of its landuse composition. The urban fringe exhibits a density of occupied dwellings higher than the medium density of the total rural-urban fringe and a higher rate of increase in population density, landuse conversion and commuting. By contrasts, the rural fringe exhibits a low density and lower rate of increase.

During the last few years different scholars have attempted to analyse some particular character of the rural-urban fringe. Young (1962)[24] studied some geographic features of the urban fringe while Morrill (1965)[25] was more specific as to the mode of its expansion. Harvey (1965)[26] considered the nature and economics of urban sprawl in general. Socio-economic problems pertaining to the fringe and fringe dwellers have attracted the attention of various scholars of this time. The study to throw light on current processes within fringe area is that undertaken by Pahl (1965)[27]. His work focuses largely upon the social character of London's fringe. He recognizes four main processes under way. There is a tendency towards social and spatial segregation, selective immigration, changing commuting character and collapse of geographical and social hierarchies.

In the less developed and developing countries, a slightly different situation has been marked. Some studies of the villages close to the major cities in these countries exhibit two main characteristics: they are closely affected by ideas and innovations flowing from the city, and they provide a permanent labour force by migration of a temporary labour force by commuting to supplement that of the city. None of these commuters are ever former urban residents. (Cornell : 1974[28] and Barclay[29], Connell[30], Rao:1970[31]. Rikkinen (1972)[32] has analysed the way in which ownership boundaries affect urban growth and landuse change, while Schonore and Klaff (1972)[33] have measured the speed of suburbanization over the last decade in the United States, compared with earlier decades.

John Hudson (1973)[34] has analysed statistically the demographic characteristics of the suburban fringe of the nine metropolitan centres in the Middle East (U.S.A.). On the other hand, in Martin's (1973)[35] study of spatial distribution of population, cities and suburbs "attention has been focused on entire metropolitan area for measuring the density gradient in which he has found a tendency for population distribution over space to vary between city and suburbs".

The initial problem to emerge from a study of the now vast scholarly literature on the urban fringe is a lack of clarity over what facts of life and landscape are under investigation (Thomas : 1974)[36]. Carter (1972)[37] feels that there are two aspects which have attracted most attention. First, there is a notion of the fringe as a distinctive area, primarily designated by characteristic landuse associations. Second, there is the notion that the social characteristics of the population of the fringe are intermediate between those of the town and those of the country.

Thus, it is clear from the above examination that the fringe is a significant development, but due to its vagueness, the areal definition of the term has not yet been standardized. However, the incoherent landuse pattern, which occurs due to outward growth process of the city, may be taken as the representative of the fringe (Lal:1973)[38]. In other words, the space into which the town extends as the process of dispersion creates the concepts of the rural-urban fringe. Golledge(1960)[39] considering all these characteristics has outlined this haphazardly developed zone of twilight as a zone of constantly changing pattern of land occupance, small farm sizes, intensive production of crops, mobile population of low and moderate density, incomplete provision of public utility services, speculative subdivision and building plots, all resulting in a continual movement or dynamism.

METHODOLOGY

From the foregoing representative definitions it is obvious that the fringe belt is a dynamic area which fluctuates in the span of time. It continues shifting outward from the city with the diffusion of urban innovations in the surrounding localities. As its development is associated with the growth of the city, it becomes more difficult to delineate this everchanging area on the periphery of a growing urban centre. However, among several researchers dealing with the fringe complex, some have discussed the systematic delineation of the fringe. Here some important methods have been examined which were used in the delimitation of the urban fringes of the different cities and towns of the world.

Mayer and Beegle (1947)[40] while distinguishing the fringe townships in the metropolitan region of Detroit used the proportionate size of the NV-RNF (Non-Village, Rural Non-Farm) population with respect to the total population of the township. The use of this index gave them the 'true fringe' consisting of township (minor civil division unit) with 50 percent or more NV-RNF population and occuring in an essentially contiguous area outside the city, where as townships with 50 percent or more NV-RNF population and occurring in an essentially contiguous area ontside the city, whereas townships with values of 25 to 50 per cent,normally farther from the city, were called 'partial fringe' areas. Rodehaver (1947)[41] in the study of Medison fringe undertook to ascertain the social, cultural and demographic characteristics of the area. The criteria used for delimiting the fringe were:

- -the percentage of non-farm families to the total number of families in a given section,
- -density of non-farm population per square mile, and
- -assessed valuation of land and buildings per acre.

By using these indices he determined the "greatest intensity zone" in respect of the surrounding area.

Blizzard and Anderson (1952)[42]delineated the fringe area of Williamsport, Pennsylvania by automobile reconnaisance and inspection method. They visualize the inner boundary of the fringe at the points where city services are not in full operation. Normally, it coincides with the corporate boundary of the city. The outer fringe boundary was placed at the approximate point where an urban pattern of living of some concentration yielded to a pattern of widely scattered acreage plots with non-farm type houses among farms, or to pure farming or forest landuses. In the Columbia fringe study, Gist (1952)[43] has selected only open country families which had one or more members employed in the city and in which residential location was at a distance of one and half miles away from the city's corporate limits. Excluded were the families in the immediate suburban zone and in villages or towns within the area. Because of certain difficulties in securing a representative sample by means of accepted sampling technique, an effort was made to locate and interview most of the urban occupied families living in the area.

Instead of using census data, Martin (1953)[44] concentrated on the specific locality, gathering first-hand data from residents of the area. His study of the Eugene Springfield fringe in Oregon was based on probability area sampling in which the location of the single family residences outside the corporate boundary and natural barriers both were considered to delineate the urban fringe. The fringe boundary was drawn at that point'where the pattern of landuse characteristics of the fringe changed to the dispersed pattern of open country farming". But he did not give any indication as to what extent the density of single family dwellings would be considered as an index of fringe characteristics. Russwurm's approach to the London (Ontario) Survey (1961)[45]was more precise and the resultant distribution more detailed. He first classified each 200 acre plots according to their residential owners or tenants engaged in non-farm occupations and then included those plots in the rural-urban fringe where 50 percent or more families were engaged in non-farm occupations. The data were obtained from the township assessors. Hind-Smith 1962)[46] in the same area identified the fringe by means of four indices: (i) land sub-divided but not yet developed or recorded by the planning board, (ii) farm lands 'for sale' for urban purposes, as indicated by realtors, (ii) land in non-farm ownerships, either idle or tenant farmed, and (iv) farm land assessed at higher than normal farm levels as shown by local assessors.

The International Urban Research Unit, University of California, following the U.S. Bureau of Census, has recommended the inclusion in the urban fringe of all those areas which have at least 65 per cent of the labour force working in economic activities other than agriculture. The fringe may be determined on this basis, but certain enclaves, departing from the above standard of the labour force, may lie. Such enclaves are the rule, rather than the exception, and, therefore, are treated as part and parcel of the urban fringe. In the study of Orlando, Florida, Mukherjee (1963)[47] has considered undeveloped subdivided land surrounding the city as fringe characteristics. The intensity of urban landuses as indicated by the sub-divisions of land and by the extent to which such sub-divisions are built-up was chosen as the major criteria for determining the urban fringe. In a recent study, Pryor Robin J. (1969)[48] has suggested a sampling frame for the rural-urban fringe. In his study, a sampling frame has been developed to meet the complex requirements of a case study of outer sub-urban and urban fringe. He used the built-up area of any city of the previous census as the inner limit of outer suburbs and present as the boundary between outer suburb and urban fringe. Outer limit of the area is fixed with the help of the sampling points taken on the vectors originating in the CBD.

In our country, some geographers have also attempted to delimit the urban fringe. U.Singh (1966)and K.K.Dube(1976)[49] have delimited the urban fringes of KAVAL Towns by superimposition of a series of maps covering several geographical factors, i.e., built-up area and house types, types and pattern of streets, occupational structures, sites for large institutions and industrial establishments, presence of lime and brick-kilns, and the limits of the essential services etc. Thus, they find that the outer limits of the primary fringes generally coincide with the municipal limits while the outer limit of the secondary fringes more or less coincides with the regulated area of these cities. Alam and Khan's (1972)[50] Metropolitan Hyderabad and its Region is one of the most outstanding work which deals with the relevant points of urban influences;and their 'metropolitan core' and 'peri-urban zone'coincide with the primary and secondary fringes of the metropolis. Nangia (1972)[51] demarcated the rural urban fringe of Delhi on the basis of 19 structural and functional characteristics. The fringe, thus demarcated, extends up to a distance of 11 to 28 kilometres, having 178 villages in total within its bounds. Further, Srivastava and Ramachandran (1974)[52] have also proved those heterogeneous factors that are responsible for the formation of present fringe of Delhi and have worked out a 'Stage Model' depicting various stages of which villages around a metropolis may pass through. Occupational structure, landuse pattern, interaction with the main city, availability of urban amenities and locational characteristics are the test variables on the basis of which the villages were ranked. The work of Phadke and Sita (1982)[53], Bore Gowda (1981)[54] Pramila Kumar (1980)[55], Sinha (1980)[56] and Hyma,B.(1971)[57] may also be cited in this regard.

DETERMINANTS TO DELIMIT THE URBAN FRINGE

It is evident from the studies that there are some common factors which may be taken as the indicators of the urban influence on the surrounding countryside. it would be a rather wise step to decide first those indices or determinants. At the same time it is not advisable to delimit the urban fringes of Indian cities on the basis of the criterion suggested for fast growing urban centres of the west. India is a developing country and its urban centres also show the same trend.

The basic factors to delimit the fringe region are concerned with landuse influx, mixed rural-urban functions, interaction with the main city, socio-economic development, availability of urban amenities and proportion of non-agricultural population. However, besides analysing each and every structural and functional characteristic in delineating the urban fringe, at least preparation of three maps of the same size, showing the present landuse, transportation and occupational pattern of the population are deemed to be helpful. In addition, personal observations in the field would go a long way in fixing the "territorial extent" of the tentative fringe upon which the said factors could be analysed.

DELIMITATION OF THE URBAN FRINGE OF BAREILLY

The studies by several authors to delimit the fringe have helped in selecting certain determinants to delineate the urban fringe of Bareilly. Here quite a few determinants have been selected which are partly spatial and partly occupational and demographic.

SPATIAL DETERMINANTS

Area of Further Extension of the Town

Based upon the landuse map (Fig.2.1) and personal investigations into the field, the possibility of further growth of the city towards different directions outside the present limit has been assumed which would be a tentative limit of the urban fringe. There is little possibility of the physical extension of the city in the adjoining south and south-west parts of Bareilly because of periodical inundation of the area by the river Ramganga and as a result thereof, the extension of built-up area along Budaun Road which runs in this direction, is negligible.

The existence of a military Cantonment lying in the south-east of Bareilly acts as a strong cultural barrier for the physical expansion of the town in this direction. Similarly, the river Nakatia flowing in the east of the city restrains the expansion of the city. Due to these factors, the development of the city along Shahjahanpur and Bisalpur Roads, running in South-east and east direction is little marked. On the other hand, with favorable geographical and economic factors the city is growing very fast towards north-west, north and north-east and most of the future development of Bareilly is expected to take place in these directions. A number of industries are developing fast in a ribbon type manner on all the three highway running in these directions due to availability of better infrastructure for industrial growth in the form of linkage and accessibility, suitability of land, etc. Industrial development is comparatively faster on Rampur Road where a continuous belt of industries has emerged up to Clutter Buck Ganj.

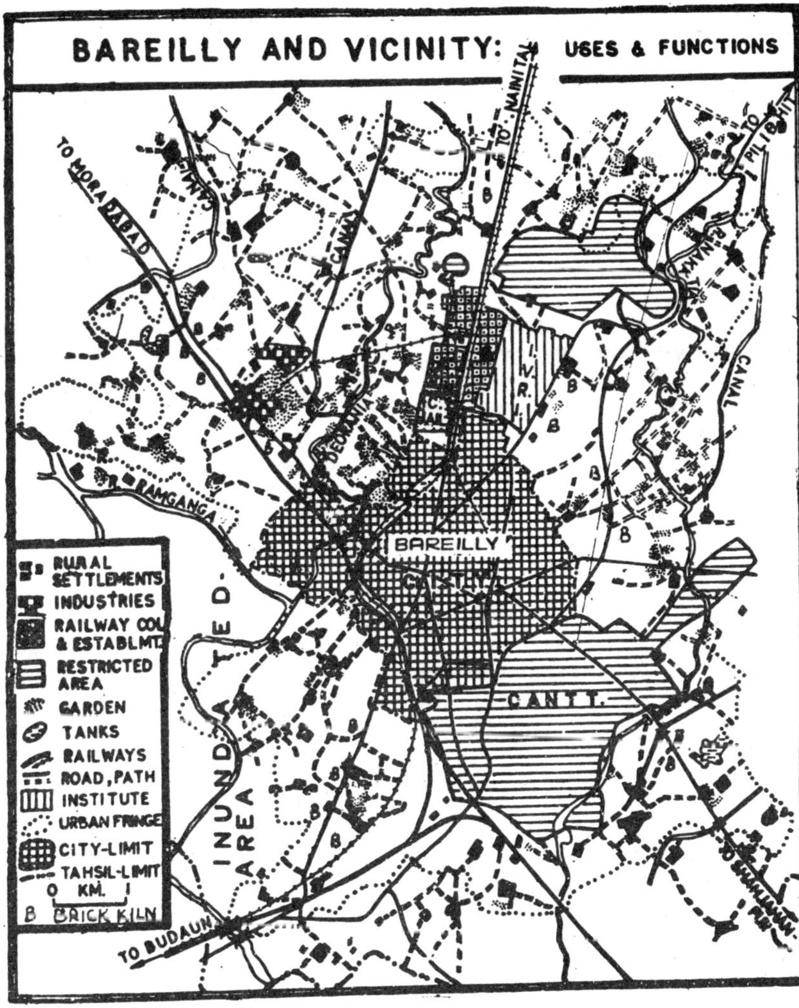

FIG. 2.1

have been recently constructed near Izatnagar on the land lying in between these roads. However, a number of settlements situated beyond the restricted area, like villages Mundia, Ahmadnagar, Chanwar, etc. on Pilibhit Road and Bilwa, Bhura on Nainital Road have strong interaction with the city.

The existing landuse pattern map reveal a mixed use of land with brick-kilns dotted along roads in plenty in the west, north-west and the north outside the city limit. Most of the villages lying in between Rampur and Nainital Roads are well connected with minor roads and are easily approachable.

Under the impact of these factors the area having strong interaction with the city is slightly linear with respect to the existing location of the city. The boundary of the urban fringe coincides with these developments. Hence, the western fringe is extended up to 10kilometres from the city centre, while it is hardly up to 7 kilometres in the southern and eastern part.

OCCUPATIONAL DETERMINANTS

Ratio of Non-Agricultural Workers:

One of the important attributes on which the impact of a city may be markedly discernible is the occupational structure of the villages. The settlements in the vicinity of the cities seem to be changing their character more conspicuously than those situated away from it. In fact, a high percentage of non-agricultural workers in the working force of the rural areas, is an approximate measure of the urban influence. This particular group is composed of the persons engaged in household and manufacturing industry, construction, trade and commerce, transport, storage and communications and in other services. These people live in areas within the orbit of cities which are classified as rural but they are not engaged in farming.

The mean percentage of workers engaged in non-agricultural occupations to total workers for Bareilly tahsil, in which the city exists, is 16.45. Villages having a greater share than the average indicates the urban influence. Hence, they have been included in the fringe region. For further grading of the intensity of this factor Standard Deviation (SD)methods seems to be helpful. Considering this mean+1SD is being taken as the lower mark for

Standard Deviation (SD)methods seems to be helpful. Considering this mean+1SD is being taken as the lower mark for fixing the outer limit of the urban fringe. For Bareilly this comes to 24.38 (mean=16.45+1 SD=7.93). Therefore, village with 24.38 or more percentage of non-farm workers have been included in the urban fringe of Bareilly. However, villages with these activities falling in value in between average and average+1 SD are taken as peripheral rural areas of rural-urban fringe. Further, in the urban fringe, villages having mean +1 SD to 3 SD's value are termed as secondary fringe while village having more value than this have been classified as primary fringe, as they show a higher degree of urban character.

When plotted on the map, the distribution of non-agricultural activities shows an extension towards the west, north, north-west and south-west. This extension is more along the roads and railway lines which provide the facility to commuters to enter the city daily for various purposes. The eastern part, with least accessibility shows a weaker influence(Fig.2.2A).

So far 31 villages come under the class'40 and above',in which 13 villages show more than 60 per cent of their working force in non-agricultural activities, while number of villages falling into 24-40 and 16-24 classes are 15 and 8 respectively.

Thus, this index gives satisfactory result and demarcate the urban fringe of the city better. On this basis, 46 villages come in closest interaction with Bareilly city.

DEMOGRAPHIC DETERMINANTS

The following determinants have been selected from the demographic structure to delimit the urban fringe of Bareilly:

Density of population:

The density of population is a fairly good index of the measurement of the influence of the city. The mean rural density for the region is 1.67 person per acre (4.12 persons per hectare) as per 1971 census. The density of population 2 persons per acre or 5 persons per hectare (it is 3 SD above the mean) has been taken as the lower limit for determining the extent of the fringe and by this 57 villages come under the fringe region. The isoline of 5 person per hectare runs

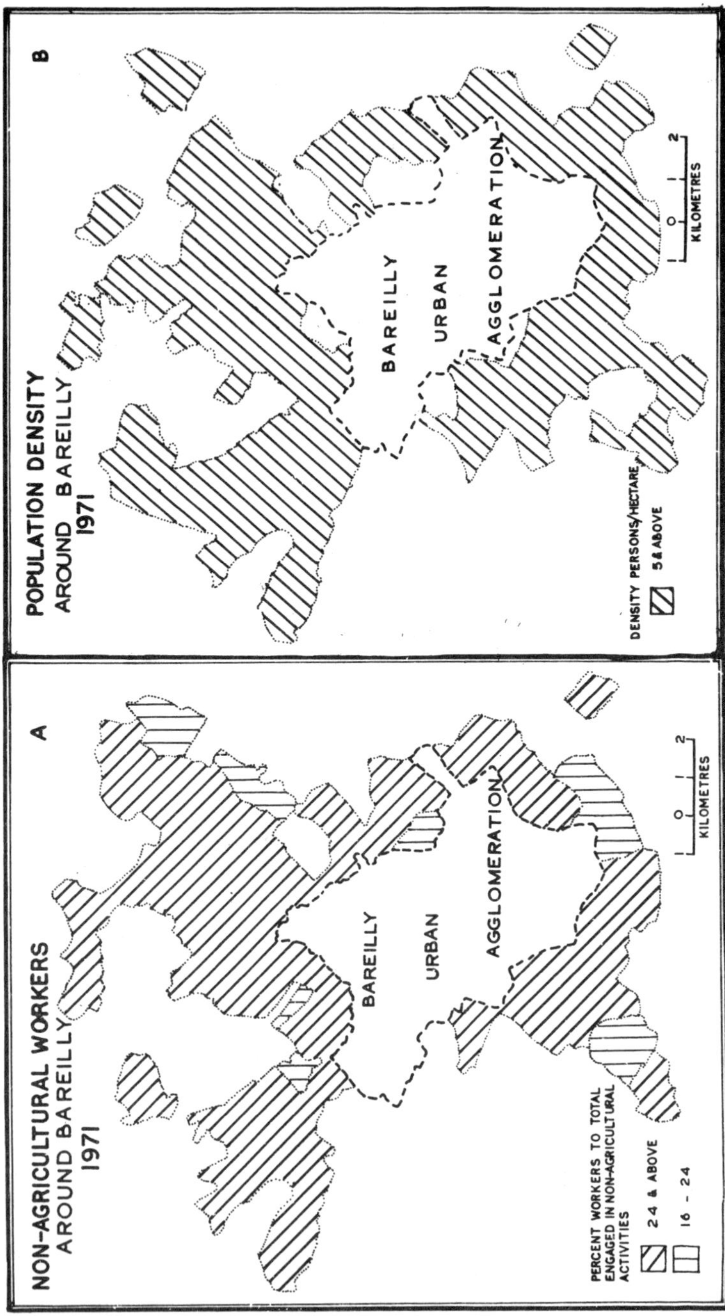
NON-AGRICULTURAL WORKERS
AROUND BAREILLY
1971
A
BAREILLY
URBAN
AGGLOMERATION
PERCENT WORKERS TO TOTAL ENGAGED IN NON-AGRICULTURAL ACTIVITIES
24 & ABOVE
16 - 24
0 1 2
KILOMETRES
POPULATION DENSITY
AROUND BAREILLY
1971
B
BAREILLY
URBAN
AGGLOMERATION
DENSITY PERSONS/HECTARE
5 & ABOVE
0 1 2
KILOMETRES

FIG. 2.2

approximately along the same distance as the previous one, with elongation towards west, north and south-west from the city(Fig.2.2B)

Rate of Change in Density

The rate of change in density during 1961-71 decade has been taken to be the other index of measurement of influence of the city. The mean change in density for the region is 26.3 and the villages showing rate above this have been taken to determine the urban fringe of Bareilly. Though this criterion provides a haphazard picture, the rate of change is more in the area situated comparatively farther from the city limit in the west. In the south also, a few villages fulfill this condition. In all, 40 villages conform to this criterion . There is a greater tendency for increase towards the north of the region as in some villages the rate of growth is more than 100 per cent. These villages are either industrial nuclei or situated near industrial suburbs (Fig.2.3A).

Population Growth:

Like density, population growth is also an important determinant for delimiting the urban fringe. 25 per cent or more growth during the years 1961-71 has been taken to delineate the fringe boundary of Bareilly. The selection of this value is based on the average growth of the tahsil. 16 out of a total of 43 villages above the average show a 50 per cent or more growth during this period(Fig.2.3B).

Sex Composition:

Incessant migration of the male population from the rural areas to the cities and their nearest settlements in search of employment increases the male population in the nearby villages. Keeping this view in mind, 800 females per thousand of male population has been selected as an index of the extent of the urban fringe of Bareilly. 42 villages situated near the city show a sex ratio of 800 per thousand males. There is a long stretch of low sex ratio in the whole northern part of the region. In 18 villages there are less than 750 females per thousand males (Fig.2.4A).

Literacy :

With the general observations that the area nearer the city will be more educated and literate than those farther

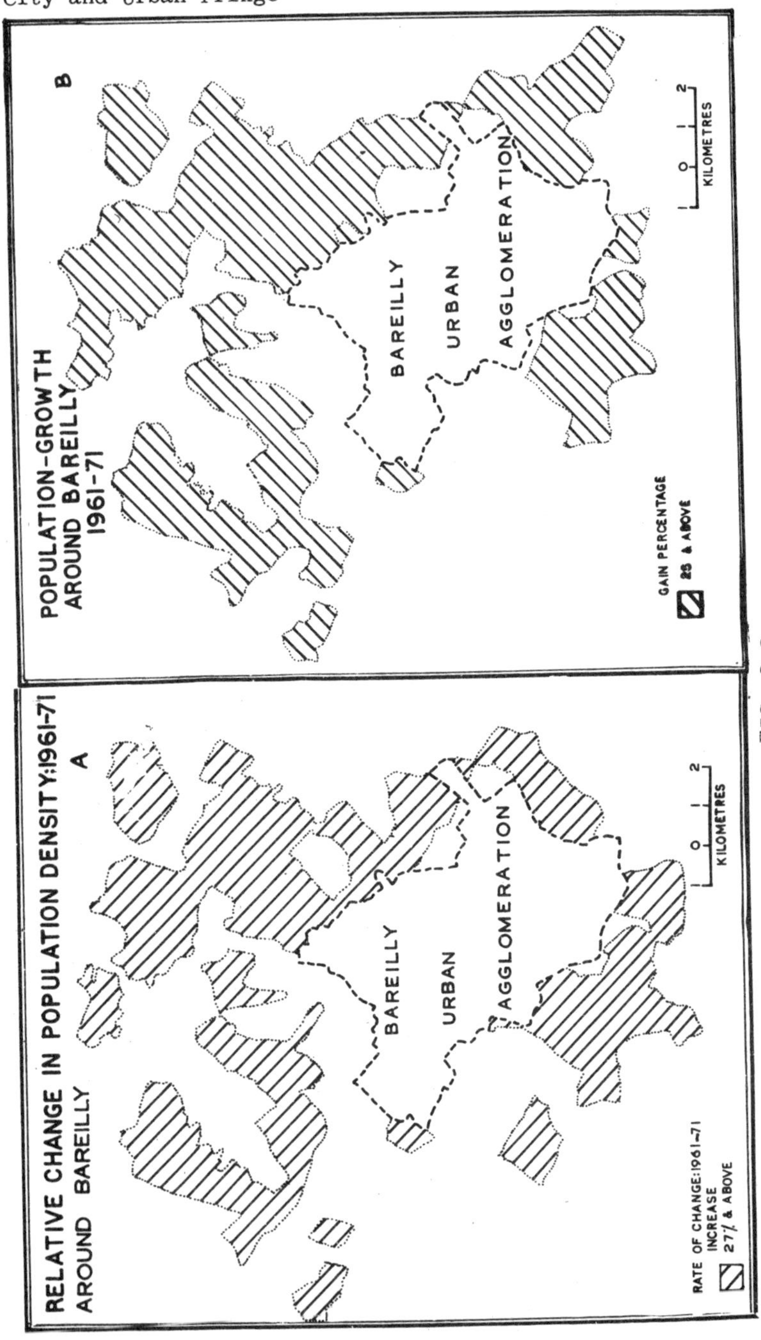
RELATIVE CHANGE IN POPULATION DENSITY:1961-71
AROUND BAREILLY
A
BAREILLY
URBAN
AGGLOMERATION
RATE OF CHANGE:1961-71
INCREASE
27% & ABOVE
0 1 2
KILOMETRES
POPULATION-GROWTH
AROUND BAREILLY
1961-71
B
BAREILLY
URBAN
AGGLOMERATION
GAIN PERCENTAGE
25 & ABOVE
0 1 2
KILOMETRES

FIG. 2.3

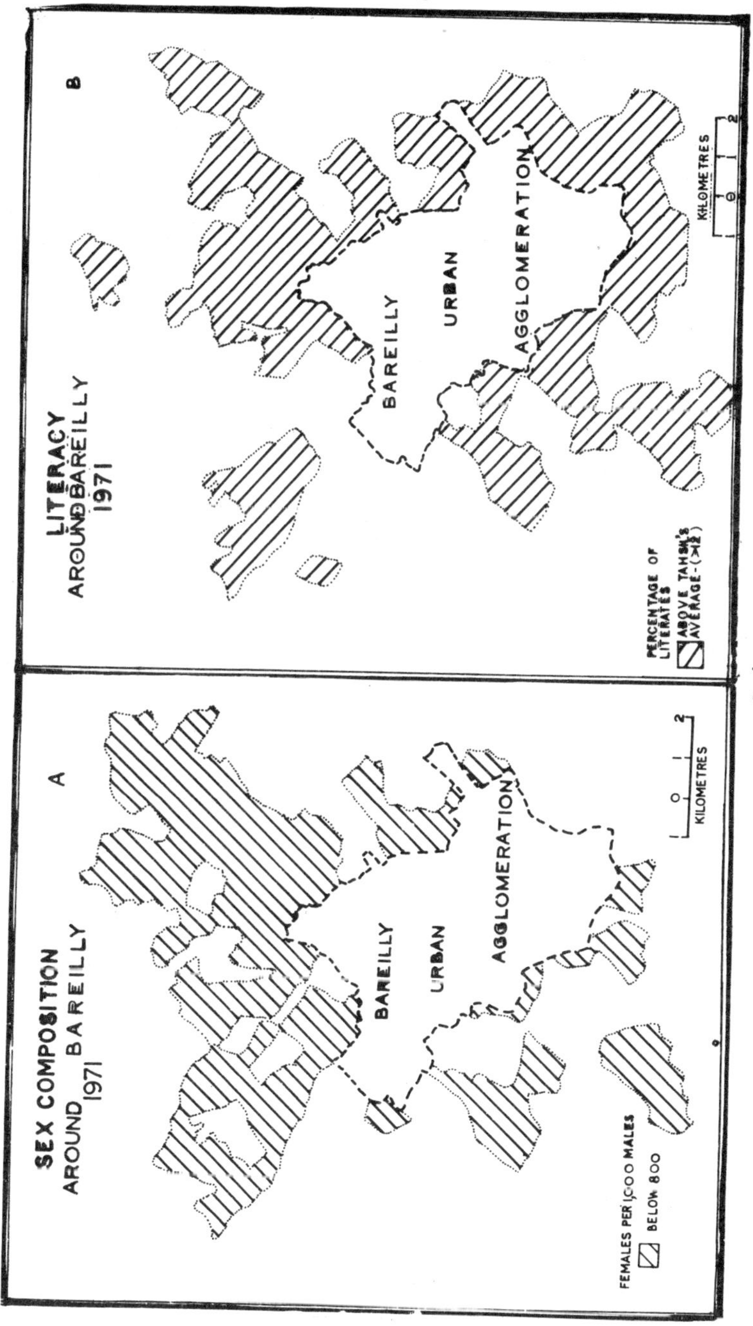
SEX COMPOSITION
AROUND BAREILLY
1971
A
BAREILLY
URBAN
AGGLOMERATION
FEMALES PER 1,000 MALES
BELOW 800
0 1 2
KILOMETRES
LITERACY
AROUND BAREILLY
1971
B
BAREILLY
URBAN
AGGLOMERATION
PERCENTAGE OF LITERATES
KILOMETRES

FIG. 2.4

away, the tahsil average 11 per cent has been fixed as the lower mark for determining the urban fringe. About 42 villages are above the average near Bareilly city in which 16 villages enjoy a much higher percentage (20 per cent or above.) The intensity of literacy is more in villages lying at the city limit than the remote villages (Fig.2.4B).

Extent and Form of Urban Fringe of Bareilly :

All these determinants when plotted on the map superimposed one over the other (Fig.2.5) provide satisfactory results. There is a zone in which most of the variables co-exist in the space and at the same time, there is also a zone where very few are conspicuous by their presence(Fig.2.6). All those villages which have fulfilled at least any three of the above indices and which are contiguous to the city, have been included in the urban fringe of Bareilly. Towards the inner side (or city), it merges into the city and towards the outerside it grades into the peripheral rural areas. The inner boundary of the fringe coincides with the municipal limits of the town that existed at the time of the previous census viz. in 1961 (Fig.2.5).

Delimited on the basis of attributes discussed above, the urban fringe of Bareilly consists of the 77 villages with an area of 134.5 Km^2(Fig.2.7). This is not a concentric zone around the city but star-shaped and it extends from 3 to 10 Km from the city. The extension of the fringe is thus approximately along the transport network, especially along the axial routes and in the inter-sectoral spaces, the fringe tends to shrink.

The urban fringe of Bareilly, thus demarcated, may be subdivided into (i)Primary and (ii) Secondary urban fringes, according to the intensity of functions. Villages having more than 30 per cent of their working force engaged in non-agricultural pursuits and fulfilling at least three of the discussed determinants have been considered as primary or true fringe. Fig.2.8 reveals the distribution of these villages in a continuous area outside the municipal limits of the city. Actually this zone is intimately connected with the city and is very important for its existence and future growth. There are 24 villages with 5521 ha. (40% of fringe area) of land which fall in this zone. The remaining 43 villages constitute the secondary urban fringe and include 7958 ha. or 60 per cent of the area of the fringe. The urban landuses and functions are, thus more prominent in the case of the former while agriculture becomes an important function in the latter.

Bareilly:Boundary - Girdle, Identification of Urban Fringe

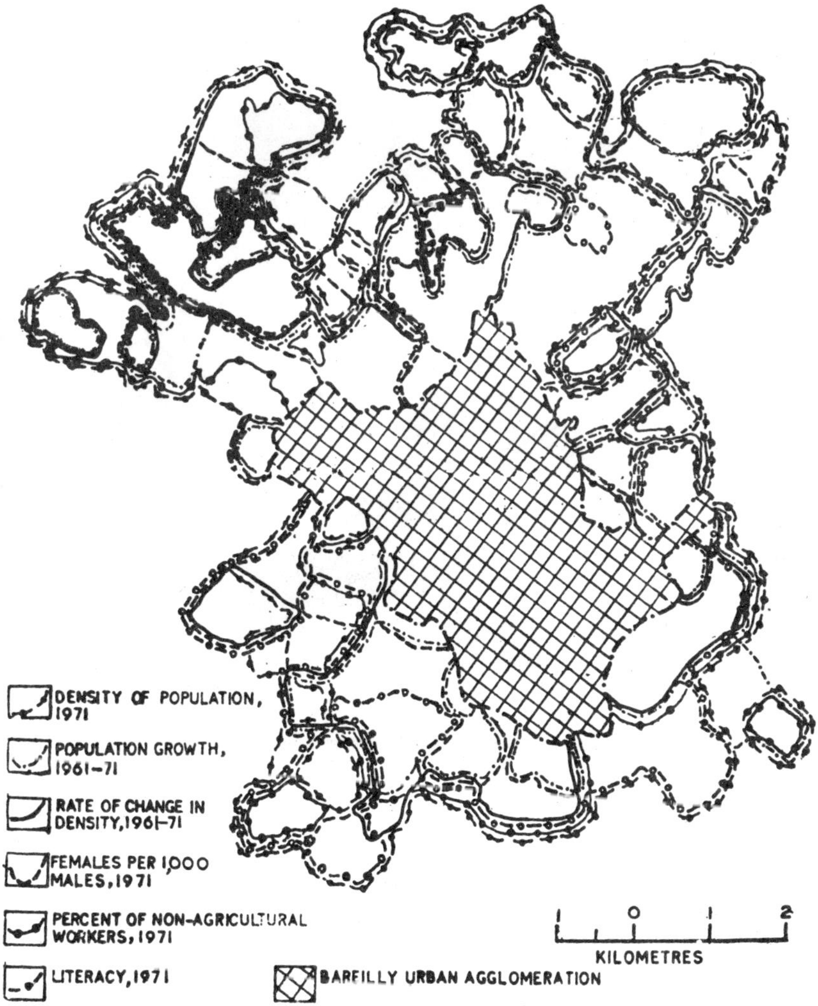

FIG. 2.5

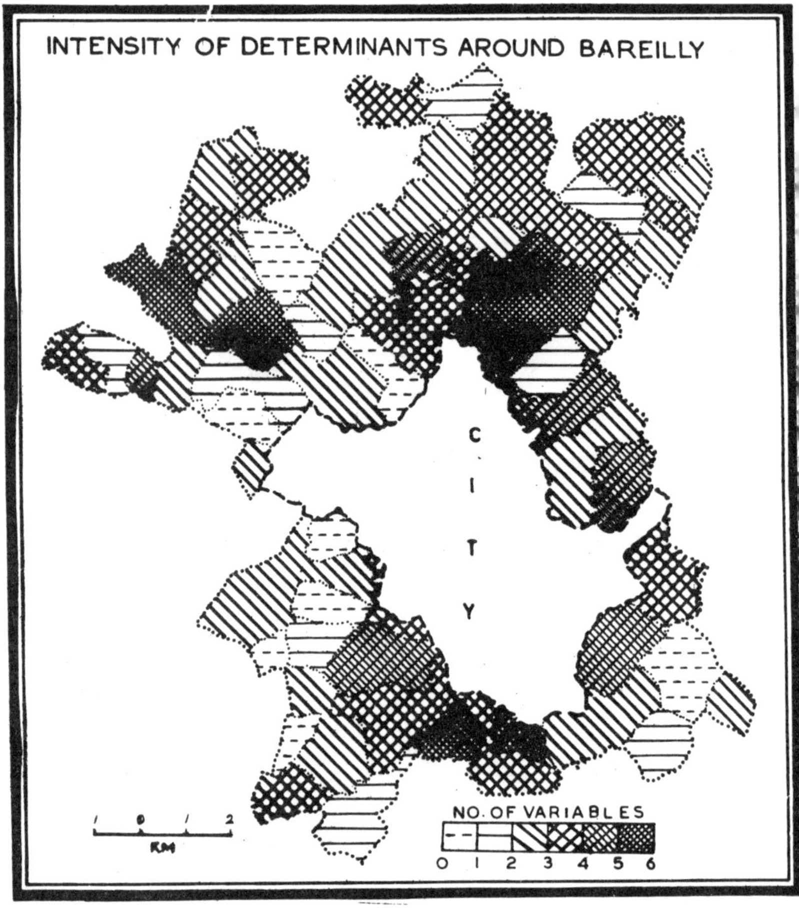
INTENSITY OF DETERMINANTS AROUND BAREILLY
C
I
T
Y
1 0 1 2
KM
NO. OF VARIABLES
0 1 2 3 4 5 6

FIG. 2.6

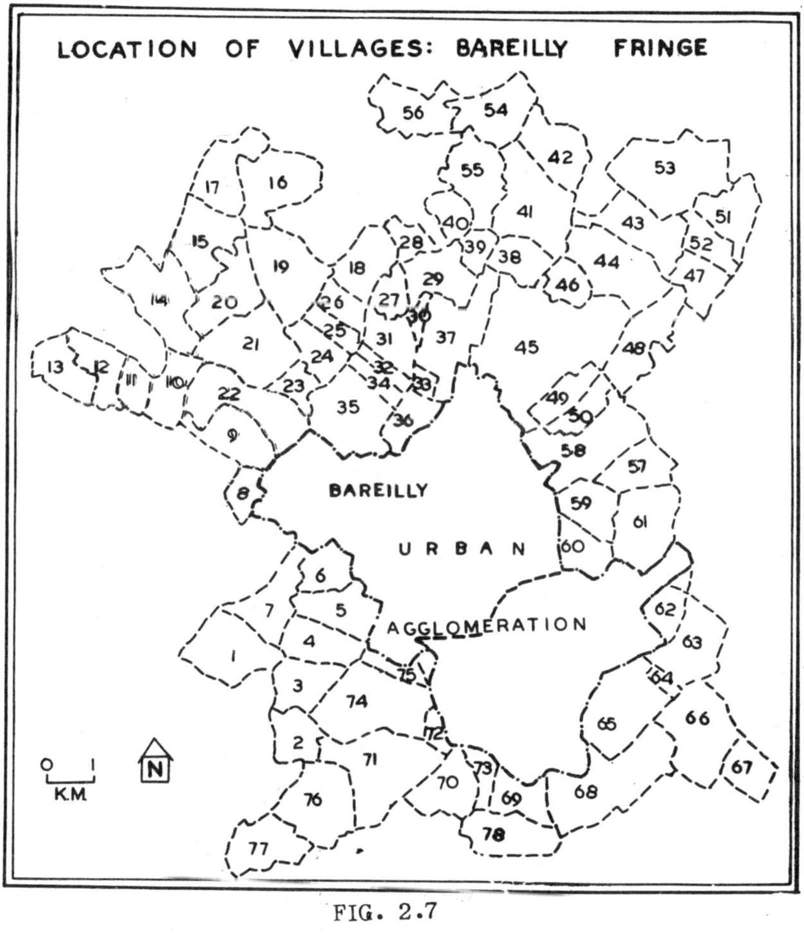
LOCATION OF VILLAGES: BAREILLY FRINGE
BAREILLY
URBAN
AGGLOMERATION
0 1
KM
N

FIG. 2.7

Urban Fringe of Bareilly: Structural Zones

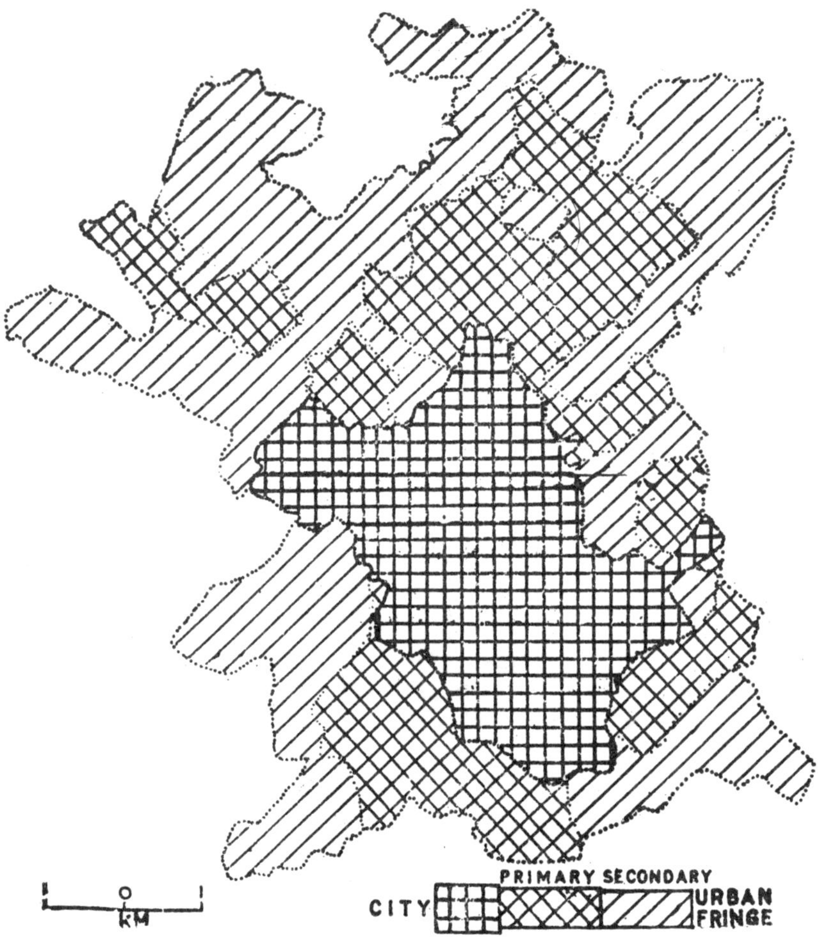

FIG. 2.3

Five villages departing from the norms also exist in this fringe. These have been included in the fringe mainly due to their nearness and technically termed as "Village enclaves". Only 10 out of the 77 villages, are being treated as "urban villages" which have partly been included in the corporate limit of city. These are undergoing a transformation process in terms of their physical, occupational and demographic structure at a much more rapid rate than the villages beyond. At the same time, they are not only facing a tremendous change in their economic structure, population growth, density and sex composition, but they have also suffered an unplanned growth of he built-up area associated with insufficient sewage and other basic urban amenities which has given rise to various problems at the edge of the city.

REFERENCES

1. T.L. Smith, "The Population of Louisiana: Its Composition and changes". **Louisiana Bulle.** No.293, 1937, p.24.
2. C.J. Gaplin, "The Social Anatomy of An Agricultural Community", **Univ. Wis, Res Bull.** No.34, 1915, p.34.
3. L.A. Salter, "Land Classification Along the Rural Urban Fringe" **Univ. of Missori Agl. Expt. St. Bull.** No.421, 1940, p.24.
4. G.S. Wehrwein, "The Rural Urban Fringe", **Eco. Geo.** Vol. 18, 1942, pp217-28.
5. R.B. Andrews, "Elements in the Urban Fringe Pattern" **Jl. of Land and public Utility Economics,** Vol. 18, 1942, pp169-83.
6. R.C. Klow, **The Park Ridge-Barrington Area: A Study of Residential Land Pattern and Problem in Suburban Chicago,** 1942.
7. F. Alpake, "Landuse Control in the Urban Fringe of Portland Orgon" **Jl. of Land and Pub. Util. Econ.** Vol.18, 1942, pp. 463-78.
8. H.H. Balk, "Urbanization of Werester's Economics" **Eco. Geog.** Vol.21, 1945, pp 104-118.
9. W.I. Fiery, "Ecological Considerations in Planning for Urban Fringes", **Amer. Social Rev.** Vol. 11, 1946, p. 411.
10. M.W. Rodehaver, Fringe Settlement as a Two Directional Movement, **Rural Sociology**, Vol.12, 1947, pp 49-57.
11. R. Dewey, "Peripheral Expansion in Milwaukee

Country" **Amer. Jl. Sociology,** Vol. 54, pp 119.
12. F. Aschman, "Dead Land", **Land Economics,** Vol. 25, pp 240-45.
13. S.W. Blizzard and W.F. Anderson, "Problems in Rural Urban Fringe Research". **Pennsylvania State College Agl. Expt. St. Progress Report,** No.89, 1952, p.11.
14. W.T. Martin, "The Rural Urban Fringe: A Study of Adjustment of Residence Location", **Univ. Oregon Studies in Sociology,** Vol.1, 1953, p.3.
15. O.D. Duncan and A.J. Reiss Jr., **Social Characteristics of Urban and Rural Communities,** John Wiley, 1956, p372.
16. R.A. Kurtz and J.B. Eicher, "Fringe and Suburbs: A Confusion of Concept, **Social Forces,** Vol.37, 1958, pp 32-37.
17. R. Golledge, "Sydneys Metropolitan Fringe: A Case Study in Rural Urban Relations. **"Aust. Geogr.** Vol.1960, pp 243-55.
18. L.H. Russwurm, "The Rural Urban Fringe with Comparative Reference to London" Referred in Alice Coleman's, **"The Planning Challenge of the Ottawa Area,** "Geogl. Paper No.42, Dept.. of Energy, Ottawa 1969, pp 11.
19. M.R.G. Conzen, "Alnwick, Northumberland, A Study in Town Plan Analysis", **Trans. Ist. Br. Geogr.,** 27, 1960, p.58.
20. G.A. Wissink, **"American Cities in Perspective, with Special Reference to the Development of their Fringe Areas"** Assen, 1962, p.201.
21. L.A. Pastalan, "Towards an Operational Definition of the Rural Urban Fringe", **Indian Social Bulln.** Vol.15, 1967, p.223.
22. J.W.R. Whitehand, "Fringe Belt: A Neglected Aspect of Urban Geography, **"Trans. Inst. Br. Geogr.,** Vol.42, 1967, p.223.
23. R.J. Pryor, "Definition of the Rural-Urban Fringe", **Social Forces,** Vol.47, 1968, pp 202-15.
—"Delineating Outer Suburbs and the Urban Fringe", **Geografiska Annaler,** Vol. 51-B, 1962, pp 1-6.
24. M.Young, "Some Geographic Features of the Urban Fringe", **The S. En. Geogr,** Vol.2, 1962, pp 1-6
25. R.L. Morril, "Expansion of the Urban Fringe : A Simulation Experiment", **Pap. Reg. Sci. Ass.** Vol. 15, 1965, pp 185-199.
26. R.O. Harvey, and W.A.B. Clark, "The Nature and Economics of Urban Sprawl," **Land Eco.** Vol.41, 1965, p. 72.
27. R.E. Pahl, **"Urbs in Rure : The Metropolitan Fringe**

in Hertfordshire", London School of Economics and Political Sciences, Geog. Pap. No.2, 1965, p. 72
28. John Connell, "The Metropolitan Village : Spatial and Social Processes in Discontinuos Suburbs" in James H. Johnson (ed) **Suburban Growth**, John Wiley & Sons, London, 1974, pp 94.
-See for example in three different areas.
29. H.B. Barclay, "Buuri al Lamaab : A Suburban Village in the Sudan, Ithaca, 1964.
30. J. Connell, "Mahmood-Abad and Telebabod Villages in Transition" in J. Connell (ed) **Semnam : Persian City and Region**, London, 1970.
31. M.S.A. Rao, **"Urbanization and Social Changes : A Study of Rural Community on a Metropolitan Fringe**, New Delhi, 1970.
32. K. Rikkinen, "Boundary Changes in a Rural-Urban Fringe Areas", **Acta Geographica**, Vol. 26, 1972, pp 25.
33. L.F. Schnore and V.Z. Klaff "The Suburbanization in the Sixties: A Preliminary Analysis," **Land Eco.**, Vol. 48, 1972, pp 23-33
34. J. Hudson, "Density and Pattern in Suburban Fringes," **Annals Ass. Amer. Geogr.**, Vol.63, 1973, pp. 28-39.
35. R.C. Martin, "Spatial Distribution of Population: Cities and Suburbs," **Jl. Reg. Sci.** Vol. 13, No.2, 1973, pp 269-278.
36. David Thomas, "The Urban Fringe : Approaches and Attitudes," Vide in **Johnson J.H. (ed)** 1974, **Op.cit**, p. 18.
37. H. Carter, **The Study of Urban Geography**, Arnold London, 1972, pp 288-296.
38. H. Lal, "Urban Fringe : An Analysis of Concept," **Uttar Bharat Bhoogol Patrika**, Gorakhpur, Vol.ix, No.2, 1973, p. 71.
39. Golledge, **op.cit.**
40. R.B.Mayers and J.A. Beegle, "Delineation and Analysis of the Rural Urban Fringe", **Appl. Anthropol**, Vo.6, 1947, pp 14-22.
41. M.W. Rodehaver, 1947, **op.cit.**
42. Blizzard and Anderson, (1952) **op.cit.**
43. N.P. Gist, "Ecological Decentralization and Rural Urban Relationship," **Rural Sociology**, Vol. 17, 1952, pp 328-35.
44. W.T. Martin, (1953) **op.cit.**
45. Russwurm, (1961) **op.cit.**
46. J. Hind-Smith, "The Impact of Urban Growth on Agricultural Land : A Pilot Survey," Referred in **A.**

Colman 1969, **op.cit,** pp 11-12. **(Ref.18.)**

47. D. Mukherjee, The Concept of Urban Fringe and its Delineation: A case of Orlando Florida," **Geogl. Rev. India,** Vol. 25, 1963, pp 53-54.
48. R.J. Pryor, "The Sampling Frame for the Rural Urban Fringe," **The Prof. Geogr.** Vol.20, 1968, pp 257-261.
49. U. Singh, "Urban Frınges is KAVAL Town," in R.L. Singh (ed) **Applied Geography,** N.G.S.I. Varanasi, 1966, pp 41-48. See also, K.K. Dube, **"Use and Misuse of Land in the KAVAL Towns",** NGSI, Varanasi, 1976.
50. S.M. Alam and W. Khan, **Metropolitan Hyderabad and its Region: A Strategy for Development",** Asia pub. House, London, 1972 pp 23-48. See also, Gopi, K.N. **Process of Urban Fringe Development: A Model,** Concept, New Delhi, 1978.
51. S. Nangia, **Delhi Metropolitan Region: A Study in Settlement Geography,** K.B.Pub. New Delhi, 1976 pp 81-102.
52. B. Srivastav and R. Ramchandran The Rural Urban Fringe **"The Indian Geogl. Jl.** Vol.XLIX, 1974 pp 1-9.
53. V.S. Phadke, & K. Sita, Delineation of the Fringe Area of an Indian Metropolis - A case study of Bombay, Paper Presented at the **'Indo-German Seminar, Hyderabad,** 1982.
54. P. Bore Gowda, Dynamic of the Rural Urban Fringe: A case study of Banglore, **Unpublished ph.D. Thesis,** Univ. of Mysore, 1981.
55. Pramila Kumar: **Agricultural Changes in Urban Fringe,** Rajesh Pub., New Delhi, 1980.
56. M.M.P. Sinha, **The Impact of Urbanization on landuse in the Rural-Urban Fringe : A Case Study of Patna,** Concept, New Delhi, 1980.
57. B.Hyma, Metropolitan Fringe Development: Madras, India, **Unpublished Ph.D. Thesis, Univ. of Pittsburg,** U.S.A., 1971.

THREE

Demographic Characteristics of the City and Fringe

GROWTH OF POPULATION IN THE CITY

Though the population figures of the Bareilly City and the Cantonment are available before 1881, they are just estimated and may not be relied upon. However, the estimated population for 1847 has been recorded as 922,08, for 1857 as 101537 and for 1865 as 105649. This shows that by 1865 the city population had risen over one lakh persons.

The 1881 census records the populations of Bareilly City and the Cantonment as 115,138 persons. The following decades (1881-1901) showed a remarkable growth in population at the rate of 15.6 per cent over 1881 figure. This was followed by little lower rate of population growth of 12.4 per cent in 1911-21 as a result of a number of epidemics followed by the World-War I. Since 1931, the city experienced a continuous rise in its population (Fig.3.1) at a considerably high rate of growth, the percentage of increase varying from 33.7 per cent during 1931-41 to 31.11 per cent in 1951-61. By 1961, the city's population had risen to over 2 lakhs. In other words, the city added about 1.5 lakhs of population within a period of one century, the average increase per year being only 1500 persons.

The growth rate of Bareilly (19.53%) in the last decade-1961-71 was much below the average growth of the urban population of the state (30.7%). But the last decade (1971-81) experienced an enormous growth of 34.25 per cent, the highest growth rate ever recorded. Amongst the first seven cities of U.P., Bareilly U.A. has the second highest growth rate after Meerut during 1971-81 as is obvious from the following table.

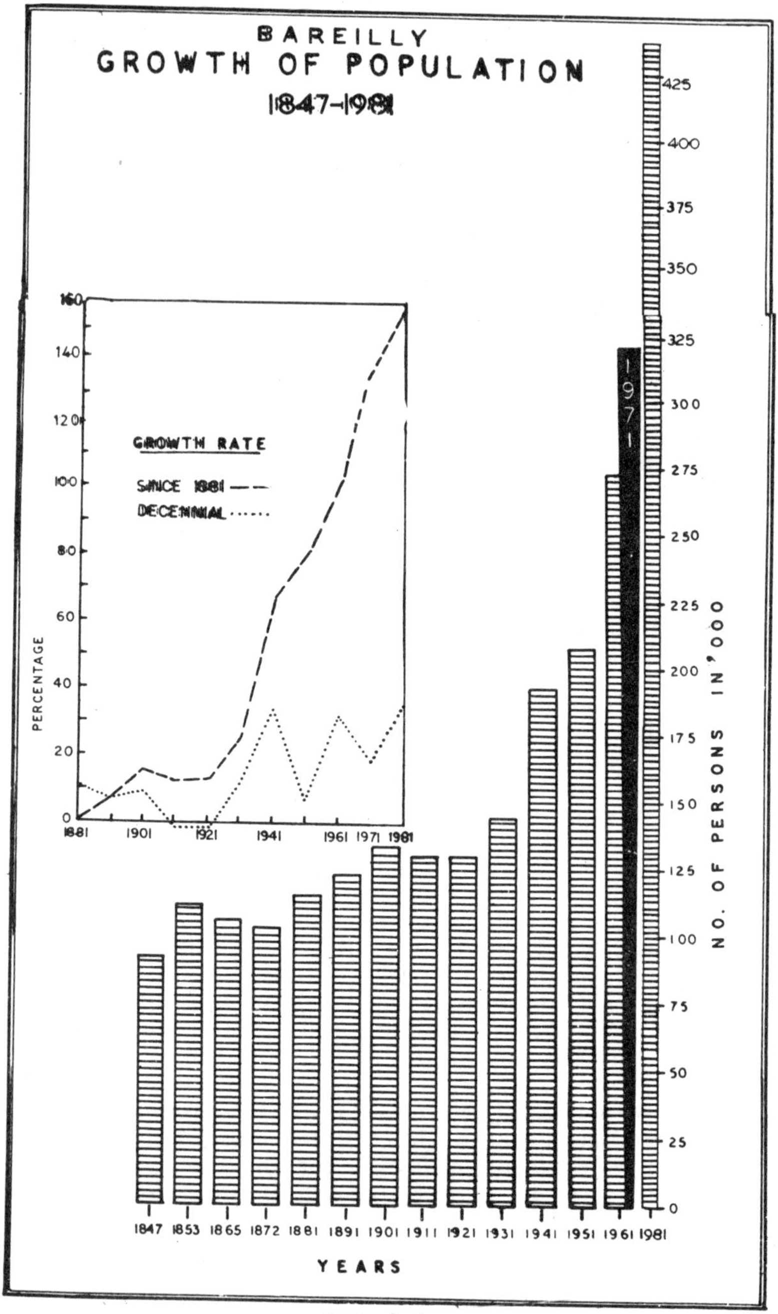
BAREILLY
GROWTH OF POPULATION
1847-1981
GROWTH RATE
SINCE 1881
DECENNIAL
PERCENTAGE
0
20
40
60
80
100
120
140
160
1881
1901
1921
1941
1961
1971
1981
1971
NO. OF PERSONS IN '000
0
25
50
75
100
125
150
175
200
225
250
275
300
325
350
375
400
425
1847
1853
1865
1872
1881
1891
1901
1911
1921
1931
1941
1951
1961
1981
YEARS

FIG. 3.1

TABLE 3.1 **Decennial Growth Rate of the First 7 Cities of U.P. (1961-81)**

Decade	Kanpur	Lucknow	Varanasi	Agra	Allahabad	Merrut	Bareilly
1961-1971	31.22	24.14	23.85	24.76	19.11	29.49	19.53
1971-1981	32.39	23.66	30.79	21.39	25.22	46.42	34.25

Source : Provisional Population Tables : Rural Urban Distribution, India, Paper 2 of 1981, pp. 178-180.

This may be pointed out here that during the last decade ending with 1981 over one lakh persons were added to city population, the average growth being over 10,000 persons per year.

The tremendous growth of population after thirties of the century is attributed to the immigration from the rural areas during the period of World War II as well as a considerable rush of dispersed persons from pakistan after partition. More than 80 per cent of the immigrants came into the city during 1947(Joshi-1968).

In the thirties and forties the population growth was caused more by natural increase than by immigration. But this trend was reversed in the following decade 1951-60 when percentage of immigration(14.7) to the city was higher than the natural increase (11.8).

TABLE 3.2 **Bareilly Population Growth**

Decades	Increase per decade	Mean decennial Rate	
		Natural Increase	Immigration percent
1921-30	10.6	10.1	0.54
1931-40	34.6	17.4	17.2
1941-50	7.6	12.0	-4.4
1951-60	26.5	11.8	14.7

SPATIAL DISTRIBUTION OF POPULATION IN THE CITY

Fig.3.2 depicts the distributional pattern of population in Bareilly in 1971. It is clear that the western middle wards, with compact built-up areas, represent the major concentration of population in an elongated shape. This ridge like span extends towards east but in lower magnitude. Kutubkhana crossing (centre of the city) shows a gap in the population distribution due to the existence of a number of public buildings.

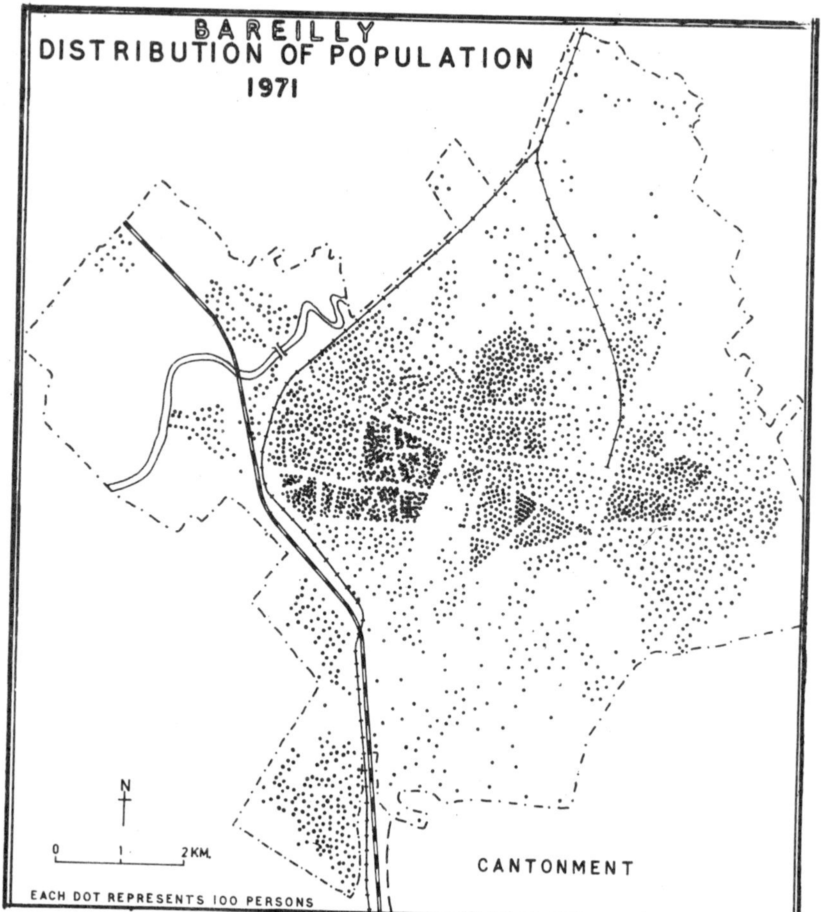

FIG. 3.2

It may be observed that distribution of population in the inner zone takes a sectoral form. It is noticeable that railway lines running at the south and western skirts of the city serve as the boundary of the high population concentration in the South-west. The main business street that divides the city into northern and southern sectors also serves as the dividing line between the old densely settled part of the city in the south and the comparatively newer sparsely populated areas in the north. Its outer limit in the north is made by a semi-circular branch railway line which connects Izatnagar with the city.

The eastern part which is known as old city, also has a compact population distribution. There is also a summit of high concentration exactly at the centre of the city covering muhallas of Shahmatganj, Kalibari and Zulfiquarganj. Besides this, there are also two small patches of high concentration at the southern newly developed part of the city. These are Nekpur, Marhinath and Subhashnagar.

The remaining parts of the city are sparsely settled. It includes Civil Lines in the south in between city and Cantonment, northern part of town including Izatnagar and Refugee colony in the west and east respectively.

Recently due to physical expansion of the city, especially in the west and east a number of villages have been incorporated within the municipal limits. These areas exhibit a typical rural setting. Surprisingly enough the villages are as congested and crowded as the main city itself.

CHANGE IN DISTRIBUTIONAL PATTERN: 1961-81.

The distributional pattern of population in 1981, shows a significant change since 1961 (Fig.3.3). During previous decades, the outer zones, especially in the north and southwest direction, have shown a continuous expansion. The Civil Lines which were very sparsely populated in 1961, with the development of several housing colonies like Rampur garden(Murtaza colony)near Bareilly college and some areas near the court, have now become an area of medium concentration.

Further, open and sparsely settled areas, beyond the branch railway track towards north, have been fully covered with houses during these two decades. Here high concentration of population can be marked on the distribution map of 1981. Similarly, in the south, areas near the railway junction have experienced a high concentration of population during this decade. Thus whole of the western and southern parts of the city have undergone a remarkable change in distributional pattern of population.

DENSITY OF POPULATION

The average density of Bareilly Urban Agglomeration was 7170 parsons per Sq. km. in 1971. But considering the builtup part of the city only, the population density rises to 21825 persons per Sq.km. The average density for different units of the agglomeration is given in the following table.

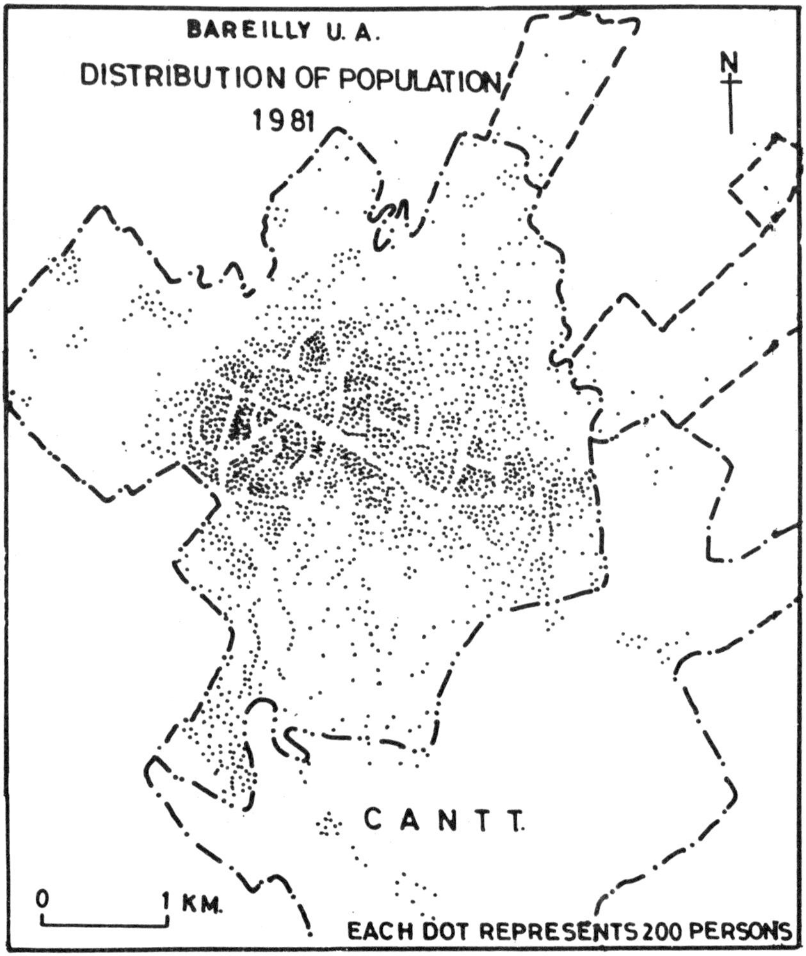

FIG. 3.3

Figure 3.4[1] reveals a high variation in the density of population in different wards of the city. The fully built up areas of the inner zones(wards No.3 and 8)show the highest density of more than 500 persons per hectare. Wards situated outside the main business areas having more open

---

1. Interpolated on the basis of Dot Map.

spaces and underdeveloped land, show a relatively lower density: below 50 persons per hectare. Here more than 75 percent of the land is unoccupied.

The wardwise population density figures represent that five wards of inner zone, namely 3,8,10,12, and 14 fall within the higher density group of more than 375 persons per hectare (Fig.3.5). These wards have approximately 8 times a higher density than the average figure for the city. Five wards surrounding these high density wards show a density ranging from 125 to 375 persons per hectare. Remaining six wards situated at the edge of the citylimit have very low density of less than 125 persons per hectare. The adjacent wards have densities more than three times the average while suburban wards (1,5 and 7) have densities loss than the average. In the north, two suburban wards namely 11 and 15 with densities above the average are exceptions as they are newly extended residential areas where many private and public residential colonies have been developed during recent years.

Cantonment by its nature is sparsely settled part of the city with a density of about 10 persons per hectare. Among planned residential areas are the railway colonies situated in the heart of the city, near the City and Junction railway stations. They present a density of 135 persons per hectare while Izatnagar railway settlement lying near the northern fringe of the city, shows a very low density of 26 persons per hectare.

VARIATION IN THE DENSITY OF POPULATION

In 1901 city's average density was 6853 persons per Km^2 but by 1931 it was reduced to 3940, mainly owing to the extension of municipal limits into large tracts of sparsely populated land. As a result, many wards of the town whose boundaries were changed, suffered a loss in their density of population in 1951 despite an actual increase in population during the period.

After 1931 city has shown a continuous growth in density which reached 9012 persons per Sq. Km. in 1981.

Analysing further on ward-basis we find that four wards situated in the inner part of the city have shown a decrease in the populations density while the remaining 12 wards have marked an increase in the decade 1961-1971 (Appendix.I). During this period maximum increase of more than 50 percent was experienced in ward Nos.1,6,10 and 12. Three out of four wards are continuous muhallas of the city. Thus, it may be noted that the outer zone recorded a much higher increase in population than the inner ones.

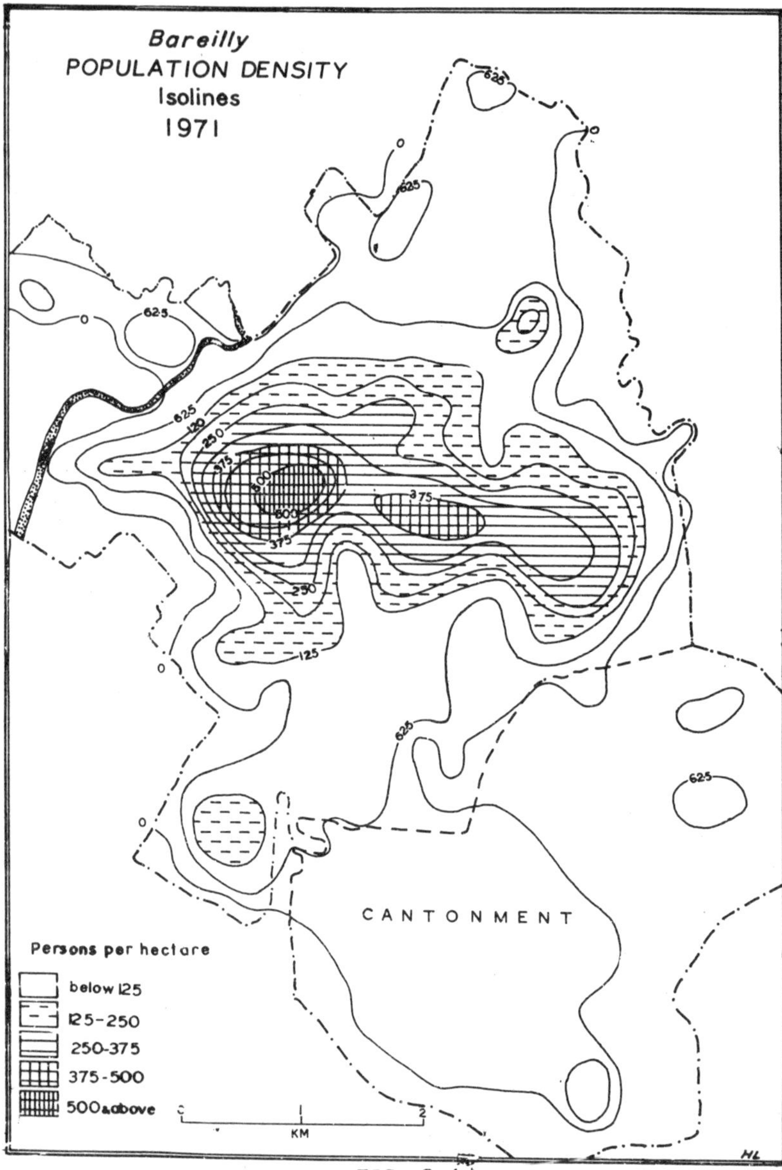

FIG. 3.4

The analysis of this growth pattern reveals that centrifugal forces are now active as the city is showing a sign of outward expansion from the compact central part due to establishment of several new residential areas on the outskirts. The Civil Lines, where the open spaces have been engulfed by several new residential colonies and other housing schemes reflected an increase of 21 percent during last decade. These recently developed planned areas, particularly in the south and north-east are credited with a low density.

TABLE 3.3 **Density of Population 1971**

	Units	Area in Km^2	Population-1971	Gross Density/Km^2
1.	Bareilly Urban Agglomeration	45.48	326,106	7170
2.	Bareilly M.B. and Nn.Rly. Colony	25.36	299,756	11820
3.	Bareilly Cantt.	17.12	18,270	1067
4.	Izatnagar Rly. Settlement.	3.00	8,080	2693

Source: Census of India, II A, 33 (1971)

TABLE 3.4 **Growth in Area and population Since 1901**

Years	Bareilly Municipal Board Area(Km^2)	Density per Km^2	Bareilly Urban Agglomeration Area (Km^2)	Density per Km^2
1901	19.43	6853	19.53	6853
1911	"	6663	"	6663
1921	"	6662	"	6662
1931	"	6905	36.55	3940
1941	"	9291	"	5272
1951	"	10019	"	5693
1961	21.60	11897	39.91	6836
1971	25.36	11820	45.48	7170
1981	23.98	15119	49.87	9012

Source : Calculated on the basis of data given in General Population Tables, PE, II-A, U.P. census, 1971, p. 183 And 1981, Series, I India, p. 492.

DENSITY GRADIENT

Gradient analysis is a quantitative technique to analyse the form of urban structure both within the city and the urban fringe. It is also an index, i.e., the ratio of gradient, to measure the centripetal pull of the city and the degree of its impact on the city-region. Spatial pattern of population distribution in an urban area can be represented for purpose of analysis in the form of a density profile originating at the city core or nucleus passing through a number of discrete points upto or beyond the urban periphery.

Usually a downward gradient is to be expected from the greatest concentration per unit area in or near the city centre towards the periphery in conformation with the negative exponential rule first proposed by Bleicher (1892). Later Clark (1951) and still later Berry, Simmon and Tennant (1963) found the rule to be satisfactory description of the density gradient observed in some hundred cities in various parts of the world, including India. The hypothesis subjected to analysis, thus is that urban population density varies inversely with distance from the city centre.

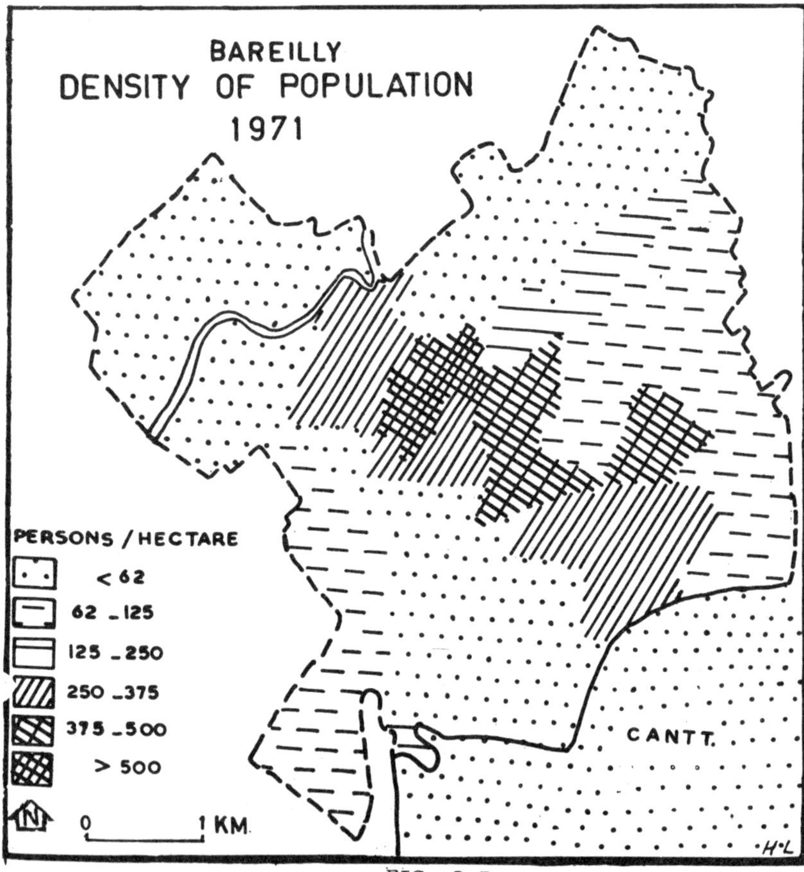

FIG. 3.5

The purpose of this enquiry is to present the intra-urban distribution of population with the help of regression analysis showing relationship between density and distance from the centre of Bareilly for 1971 census. The areal pattern has further been analysed by mapping residuals from regression equation using Brush Model.

REGRESSION ANALYSIS[2]

The analysis of data for Bareilly gives a correlation coefficient of -.83 a coefficient of determination of .69 and F ratio exceeding the one per cent level(Table 5). Thus the relationship of density to distance in Bareilly is of high statistical significance. In other words, this result of analysis shows a good fit of the linear regression model and lie well within the range of the previous findings of other researchers. The regression of population density in the present town yields a figure of 483 persons per hectare at the point of origin and a rapid decline to less than 70 at two Kilometers and 11 persons at 3.5 Kilometers

DEVIATIONS FROM REGRESSION

A simple linear regression does not adequately describe the population varient as well as the observed population pattern. A line with two inflections known as the confidence limit or Standard Error of estimate (Sxy) is more significant than the straight line obtained by simple regression analysis. The trend of these deviations from regression is shown clearly by calculating density according to distance increment as seen in the graph (Fig.3.6). Within the first half of a Kilometre the density curve is below the regression line. Again after showing a short fall below the regression the trend is reversed and density now rises above the regression line upto city limit.

The municipal wards tend to cluster at about 350 to 550

---

2. Methodology - After drawing successive circles of half Kilometer intervals from Kutubkhana, the city centre, population of each belt is aggregated by counting number of dots on a distribution map and the density values are computed accordingly. Now these data are treated in terms of linear regression: Y=a+bx, where Y is the population density expressed as the number of persons per hectare: a is a constant and b is a variable, both derived from the density data and x is the distance, expressed in Kilometres.

persons per hectare within the first kilometer with some of them lying above and beyond the confidence limit. Peripheral wards' density diminishes markedly and in many statistical units it falls well below the confidence limit.

Another feature worthy of note on the graph to the right is that maximum density of population does not occur in the central core, although it is reached within half a kilometer radius. A striking feature in Bareilly is the sharp drop in density from over 400 persons per hectare in the main city to less than 50 immediately outside it (Table 6).

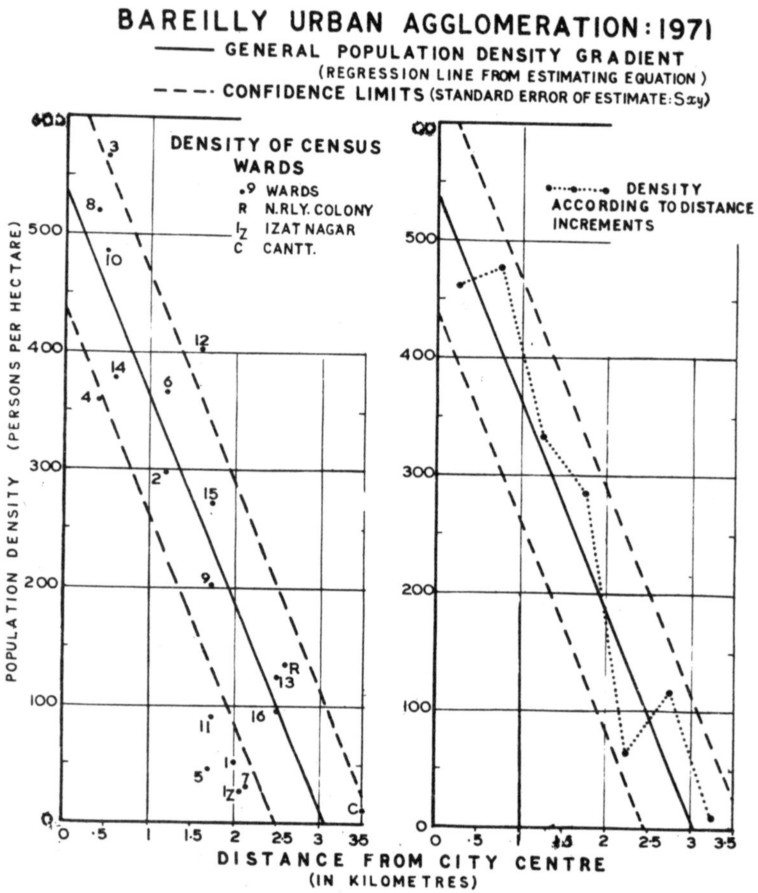

FIG. 3.6

TABLE 3.5 **Regression of Population Density in Bareilly Urban Agglomeration-1971**

No. of Statistical Unit : 19

Estimating Equations:		
	Regression coefficient (b)	= -176.3
	Base constant (a)	= 540.6
	Standard Error of Estimate (Sxy)	= 102.8

Wards	Km. from city	Density Persons/Hectare	
1	2.0	52	
2	1.2	298	
3	0.5	568	
4	0.4	360	$r = -.83$
5	1.7	46	$r^2 = .69$
6	1.2	368	Significance
7	2.2	32	of F ratio :
8	0.4	520	(F, Ratio exceeds
9	1.7	203	one percent level
10	0.5	485	of probability
11	1.7	91	
12	1.6	403	
13	2.5	124	
14	0.6	381	
15	1.7	271	
16	2.5	95	
Cantt	3.5	11	
N.Rly Colony	2.6	135	
Izatnagar	2.1	22	

Source : Computed on the basis of census data.

TABLE 3.6 **Variation in Population Density by distance increase in Bareilly urban Agglomeration: 1971**

Distance Zones Km. From city Centre	Density Persons/ hectare
0.0 - 0.5	483
0.5 - 1.0	478
1.0 - 1.5	333
1.5 - 2.0	285
2.0 - 2.5	66
2.5 - 3.0	118
3.0 - 3.5	11

$r = -.96$, $r^2 = .93$

Source: Computation by Author.

RESIDUALS FROM REGRESSION

Mapping residuals from regression equations provides a means by which the relationships among phenomena can be seen in their areal setting. It makes possible to see more clearly the degree to which the actual patterns deviate from the regression model.

Fig.3.7 compares the actual urban density (Fig.3.5) with the density that would exist if population held exactly to its general linear relationship with distance (Y=-176 x + 540)(Table-7). The most extensive areas of positive departure on both maps are in the area generally north of the main business street and in the eastern part of the town. The wards (3 and 12) situated in the central part of the old and new town with highest density show highest positive resideuals. That is, these are the only statistical units where the residuals rise above the standard error of estimate.

TABLE 3.7 **Residuals from Regressionof Population Density, 1971**

Wards	X	Y	Y'	Z(Y-Y')	Z^2	$\frac{Y-Y'}{Y}$ X 100
1	2.0	52	188	-136	18496	-261.53
2	1.2	298	328.8	-30.3	948.6	-10.33
3	0.5	568	452	116.0	13456.0	20.42
4	0.4	360	469.6	-109.6	12012.2	-30.44
5	1.7	46	240.8	-194.8	37947.0	-423.40
6	1.2	368	328.8	39.2	1536.60	10.65
7	2.2	32	152.8	-132.8	17635.8	-415.00
8	0.4	520	469.6	50.4	2540.2	9.69
9	1.75	203	232.0	-29.0	841.0	-24.28
10	0.5	485	452.0	33.0	1089.0	6.80
11	1.75	91	232.0	-141.0	19881.0	-154.94
12	1.6	403	258.4	144.6	20907.2	35.88
13	2.5	124	100.0	24.0	576.0	19.35
14	0.6	381	434.4	-53.4	2851.6	-14.01
15	1.75	271	232.0	39.0	1521.0	14.39
16	2.5	95	100.0	-5.0	25.0	5.26
NR	2.6	135	82.4	52.6	1766.7	38.96
IZ	2.1	27	170.4	-143.4	20503.5	-531.11
C	3.5	11	+76.0	-87.0	4225.0	-790.90

$$Z^2 = 179821.52$$

$$S_Y = \sqrt{\frac{Z^2}{N}} = 97.284$$

X = Distance in Km; Y = Density, persons/hectare
Y' = Expected Value of Y when Y = -176x + 540, Sy = Standard Error of Estimate=97.3
Z = Residuals

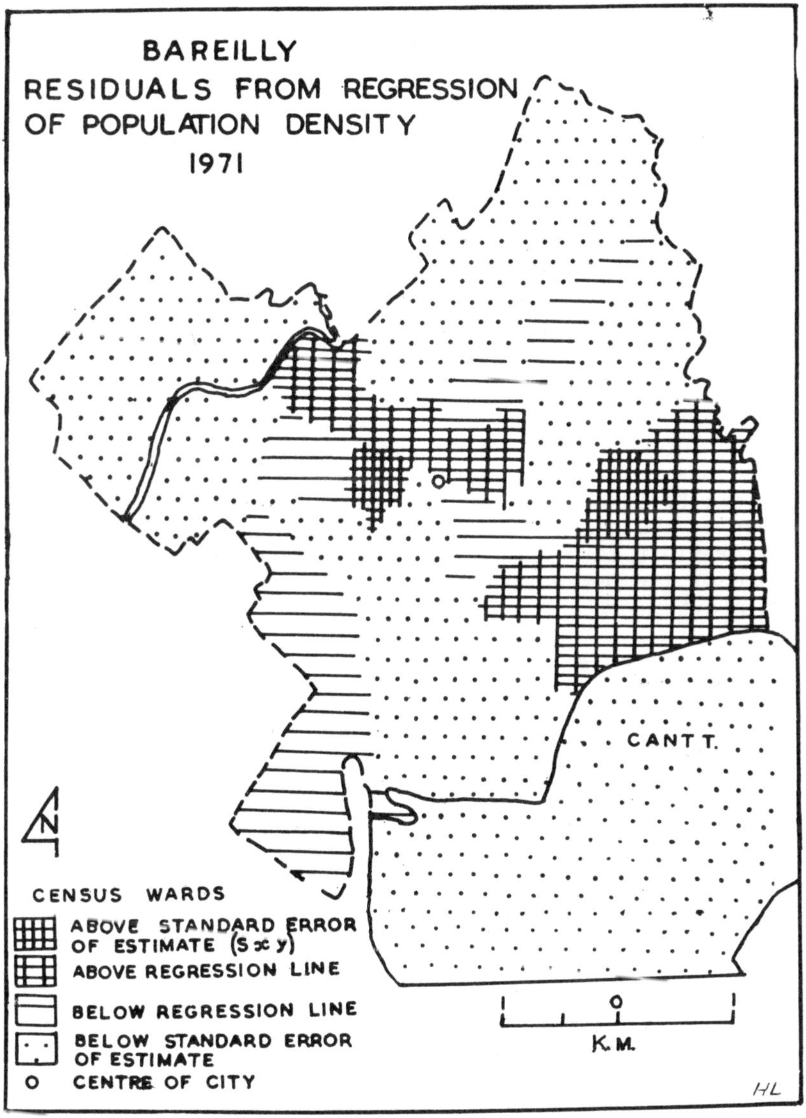
BAREILLY
RESIDUALS FROM REGRESSION
OF POPULATION DENSITY
1971
CANTT.
N
CENSUS WARDS
ABOVE STANDARD ERROR
OF ESTIMATE (Sxy)
ABOVE REGRESSION LINE
BELOW REGRESSION LINE
BELOW STANDARD ERROR
OF ESTIMATE
CENTRE OF CITY
0
K.M.
HL

FIG. 3.7

Major areas of negative residuals are distributed in the southern half of the town particularly on the western portions which coincides with comparatively scattered settled Civil Lines and newly extended wards.

The Çantonment, Civil Lines and areas near Shahdhana Rly. Station and Izatnagar area (North and North-east) plus Baquarganj in the west, Townhall and Beharipur in the central wards are the the areas with relatively low density falling below the regression line and in several wards below the standard error of estimate. All these areas except some parts of ward number 4, are newly settled areas of the city and contain several new public and private residential colonies of moderate (average) density. Ward number 4, though lying in the heart of the town, shows a major portions of its land used as Government building, i.e.Townhall, Govt. Inter College and its open field. Likewise, Baquarganj area has most of the inundated land in its limit which is partially inhabited. The negative departures that occur in most of the southern and north-western portions of the town may reflect more extensive type of landuse. Thus, the pattern of the depaertures from regression is assymetrical in this city.

URBAN POPULATION COMPOSITION

AGE-SEX COMPOSITION

Age pyramids of Bareilly (Fig.3.8) clearly reveals a high proportion of the total population in the working age-group of 15-59 years in 1971. The following table shows that about 54 percent males and 51 percent females fall in this age-group. On another hand, male population in the non-working age-group (less than 15 and above 60) is lower than that of the female population.

The same trend is marked in the age structure of fringe population as indicated in the same table No. 8.

The **sex ratio** is a suitable demographic indicator reflecting the population composition of the area and the economic and social implications there of. It is interesting to note that male female ratio in Bareilly urban agglomeration remains morecless the same (843) for the last four decades (Table 9). However, it has always been higher than the average figure for urban area of the State till 1971.

TABLE 3.8 **Bareilly-Age Sex Composition : 1971**

Population	Below 15 yrs.	15-59 years	above 59 years	All ages
Bareilly U.A.				
Male	40.8	53.7	5.5	100
Female	44.0	51.0	5.0	100
Male + Female	42.4	52.3	5.3	100
Bareilly Fringe:*				
Male	43.3	49.2	7.5	100
Female	42.8	51.4	5.8	100
Male + Female	43.0	50.3	6.7	100

* Based on personal survey sample data, 1974

TABLE 3.9 **Change in Sex-Ratio**

Years	Bareilly	Urban Areas of U.P.
1921	817	826
1931	814	807
1941	819	805
1951	844	820
1961	841	812
1971	843	821
1981	843	846

The fig. 3.8 further indicates that though there was little variation in sex ratio on ward basis during 1961, a considerable evenness is being marked in 1971. Ward No. 3, an old settled part of the city, presents a higher sex ratio (902 in 1971) in both the census years while most of the suburban wards including Civil Lines have moderate sex ratio of about 800 females per thousand of males. Cantonment consisting of a large number of military establishments and generally employing males, represents the lowest sex ratio, ie. 580 females per 1000 males.

OCCUPATIONAL STRUCTURE

Pattern of occupational structure of Bareilly compares favourably with that of Kanpur. Obviously Kanpur being the industrial city of the state engages the highest percentage (30%) of its workers in manufacturing while the corresponding figure for Bareilly is only 22 (Table 10). Manufacturing combined with household industries ranks first in the occupational activities of this urban agglomeration. Next to industry come other services engaging about 27 percent of the workers. Trade and commerce employ 18 percent, while transport engagesd 17 percent of the working population. Among the first seven cities of the state, Bareilly has the highest proportion in the constructional activities (about 4%). Only 5.6 percent of the workes are engaged in primary activities.

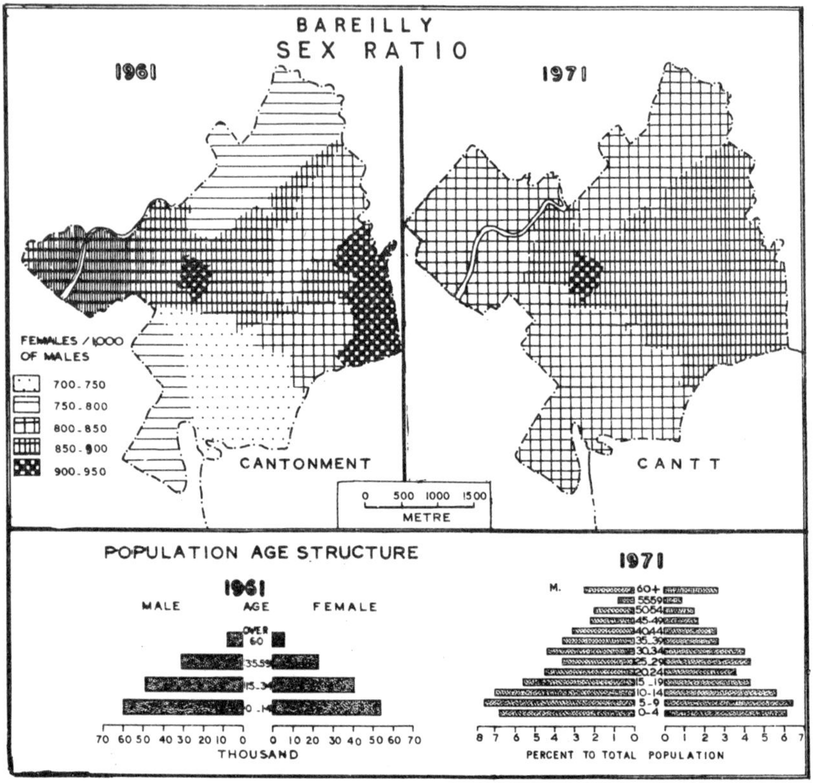

FIG. 3.8

Using the standard deviation method of classification of towns, the city is characterized as multifunctional and it falls in the category of 'Industry-cum service-cum commercial town.

TABLE 3.10 **Occupational Structure of the First 7 cities of U.P. 1971**

Urban Centres	Agriculture & allied	Household Industries	Manufacturing Industry	Construction	Commerce	Transport	Other services
Kanpur	4.8	4	30	1.2	21	9	30
Lucknow	5.0	4.5	16	1.5	18	14	41
Varanasi	2.5	25	13	1.5	22	10	26
Agra	6.7	8	24	0.3	22	12	26
Allahabad	9.5	5	14	1.5	18	9	43
Meerut	1.6	6	20	2.4	19	10	42
Bareilly	5.6	5.6	22	3.8	18	17	27

CHANGES IN LIVELIHOOD PATTERN

The generalized picture given in the following table (Table-11) indicates the changes in the livelihood pattern of Bareilly since 1901. It may be observed that agriculture as a means of livelihood has declined to 5.6 from 10.7 percent. A little increase in percentage in 1971 over the previous decade in this regard is mainly due to the inclusion of a number of villages in the municipal limit in 1968.

TABLE 3.11 **Trend of Occupational Structure 1901-1971**

Occupation	Percent of workers						
	1901	1911	1921	1931	1951	1961	1971
1. Agriculture & Allied	10.7	8.2	8.0	6.8	4.1	3.4	5.6
2. Industries	29.9	27.0	23.2	24.0	24.9	28.0	27.6
3. construction	2.7	2.5	2.4	2.8	2.4	4.2	3.8
4. Trade & Commerce	16.7	14.3	15.0	15.0	19.2	18.5	18.0
5. Transport	4.1	6.6	6.0	8.7	11.8	14.5	17.0
6. Other services	35.3	41.4	45.4	41.2	37.6	31.4	27.0

Transportation has shown a regular increase during the last four decades while industry and other services have maintained their high percentage during all the six decades.

SPATIAL VARIATION OF OCCUPATION WITHIN THE CITY

Fig. 3.9 shows the ward-wise detailed occupational structure of Bareilly in 1971. It is evident that peripheral wards are still having more workers engaged in agriculture than the central wards of the city. In ward Nos. 1, 6 and 13 this group occupies 13 to 16 percent of working population of the area (Appendix II). This is due to the existence of a number of villages dotted in the suburban zones. Persons engaged in trade and commerce are generally clustered together in the central part of the city well connected with the industrail areas by a number of roads. Ward No. 5, 16 and Contonment are the areas of maximum concentration of people engaged in services. However, almost all the wards have high percentage of their workers engaged in this category ranging from 20 to 48 percent. In addition to northern Railway colony and Izatnagar outgrowth, transportation is the main occupation including wards Nos. 1, 11 and 16 where all three railway stations are located.

Ward Nos 1o and 12 situated in the Inner zone of the city shows a considerable fraction of workers in household industries, especially in furniture making. Thus a segregation of functions and occupaional zoning have developed in the city in relation to the nearness of one's place of work.

ECONOMIC ASPECT OF THE OCCUPATIONAL PATTERN

In Bareilly, the average participation rate is 26.6 percent of which 96.7 percent are males and only 3.3 per cent are females. Out of a total population of 326,106 persons in 1971 as many as 239,264 persons (73 percent) wre classed as nonworkers out of whom about 61 percent were females and 39 percent males. In conclusion, the occupational structure of the city is characterized by the predominance of nonproductive male population comprising of a large number of dependents.

LITERACY

The total literate population of Bareilly was estimated at 41.2 percent in 1971 as against state's urban literacy (50%). This ratio has increased to 46.86 percent in 1981. There exists a great variation in the percentage of literacy from ward to ward ranging from 20 percent in the newly extended wards number 1 and 13 to more than 60 percent in the centrally located wards and peripheral railway colonies (Fig. 3.10). The literates and the total population of the wards of the city indicate a high positive correlation of coefficient (0.76). As this centre comes under Industry-cum Service-cum comemrcial functional group, most of the wards are occupied by persons engaged in services and business which in turn enhances the literacy percentage in general.

POPULATION CHARACTERISTICS OF THE URBAN FRINGE

Growth Rate : Bareilly fringe registered a phenomenal

growth of population during the past two decades. An examination of the tendencies of population growth in Bareilly and its urban fringe (Table 12) during 1951-61 indicates that though the growth rate of the Bareilly Urban Agglomeration has been more than the Bareilly Municpal Board, not many of the fringe units have grown faster than the core city. There were only 5 villages which registered a growth rate higher than that of the central city. While during 1961-71 about 50 percent of the fringe villages registered a higher rate of growth compared to the central city. The populaion of Bareilly Urban Agglomeration increased by 19.5 percent during this period whiloe its fringe registered a growth rate of 31.02 percent. Figures reveal the fact that there is a direct relationship between population growht and the main economic activity of the area. Fringe villages with industrail establishments are having a much higher growth rate : Khalilpur-Clutterbuckganj (95.0%) and Biharman Nagala (79.81%).

TABLE 3.12 **Variations in Population in Bareilly and its Urban Fringe : 1951-71.**

	Total Population			Percent Variation	
	1951	1961	1971	1951-61	1961-71
City	208283	272828	326127	31.11	19.53
Fringe	60371	81502	106795	35.00	31.03

Source : Compiled from 1951, 1961 1971 District Census Hand books for Bareilly.

TABLE 3.13 **Variations in Population Growth and Density in the Fringe according to distance.**

Distance Km. from city Centre	Percent rate of change in population growth 1961-71	Rate of change in density - 1961-71 (per hectare)
3-4	3.17	2.89
4-5	35.72	35.78
5-6	16.44	16.41
6-7	40.21	40.42
7-8	34.33	34.92
8-9	31.41	30.98 r= -0.58

Distance and direction from the city do have some bearing in this context. Villages lying at the immediate edge of the city present a minimum rate of change (3.17 percent) (Table 13) while maximum increase has occurred between 5 to high population-growth tends to centre towards the north and north-west. Elswhere, the high population growth has been observed in a scattered form, mostly in and near the villages having any kind of industries within their limits. On the contrary, there are vilages recording negative population growth also. Such units include those bordering villages, which have been partly included in the city during recent years and their remaining parts are either marshy or low lying ill-drained areas. A narrow strip of such villages can be seen in north-eastern border of the city while another small patch is located on the eastern border. Much of the region, however, has shown a growth between 25 and 50 percent in its population (higher than the average population growth of the Tahsil as well as the country) but this is not a continous zone.

Areas experiencing less than 25 percent growth in their population are either confined to the secondary fringe or low-lying areas along the reiver. A narrow continous strip with low population growth exists in the west along the river Deorania, through eastern bank of the Ramganga which extends upto the city limit. The reason behind this low growth may be attributed to the distance factor from the main highways as well as their situation in the inudated areas.

Barrina a few exceptions, the settlements near the city and connected by good roads have recorded enormous growth. Hence, with the onset of industrialization and resultant modern development in the city in the early 1960s and the concomitant emergence of clusters on the fringe of the city, the pace of growth of the fringe in general has gained momentum.

Simple linear function fitted to the growth data indicates a substantial relationship between population growth and the distance from the city centre : $r = -0.58$ and $r^2 = 0.33$; in other words 33 percent of the variation in population growth is due to distance (Table 13).

DENSITY OF POPULATION

The average density of population in the urban fringe of Bareilly was about 8.32 persons per hectate in 1971, which is almost twice the density of district's average (4.12). The corresponding figures in 1961 decade were calculated to be 6.5 and 3.8 indicateing that the density has increased at a much faster rate in the fringe than the district as a whole. The villages of the urban fringe show great variations in the density of population. At places it is as high as 42 persons per hectare and the lowest figure comes to about 1.0 person per hectare. The areas of maximum populationdensity exist in the north-western and south eastern inner parts of the fringe (Fig. 3.11-A). These places are either along the transport routes or near the municipal limit. However, the accessibility of these villages appears to be a significant factor causing variations in the population density.

Most of the outskirt villages of the north and north-east part of the fringe, virtually lying in the secondary fringe, present low to medium (below the average of district's rural) density. Same pattern is also visible in the southwest portion. The villages, on the other hand, lying at the municipal limit, exhibit very low density of below 5 persons per hectare. These low density areas are characterised by either least accessibility or higher percentage of cultivable fields and open waste lands of the villages included in the city.

CHANGES IN DENSITY PATTERN : Considering distance, further variations may be observed. The distance-density curve for the fringe shows decline towards rural areas and the rate of decline varies from one distance zone to another. The zone between 6 to 7 km. of distance has shown maximum density in both the census years (12.5 persons in 1971 and 8.7 persons in 1961) while it is minimum in the outer zone.

A similar trend, though different in magnitude, occurs along the main routes. In Bareilly-Rampur ribbon (in the West) a steeper density gradient is visible after 5 km. distance from the centre; i.e. from 30 to 7 per hectare. This ribbon has a very high population density (18 persons).

In conclusion, the density of population has shown an overall increase from 1961 to 1971. It has shown a greater tendency to increase towards the north-west than towards the east and south of the region.

SEX COMPOSITION : The influx of in-migrants into the urban reas lowers the ratio of male-female composition of population. Since most of these are unskilled labourers or semi-educated persons suitable only for lower cadre jobs they stay in the semi-urbanized environment or nearb y surrounding villges and consequently nearer the city male population tends to exceed the female population. There is a long stretch of low female ratio on the whole north-western part of the fringe (Fig. 3.12 A).

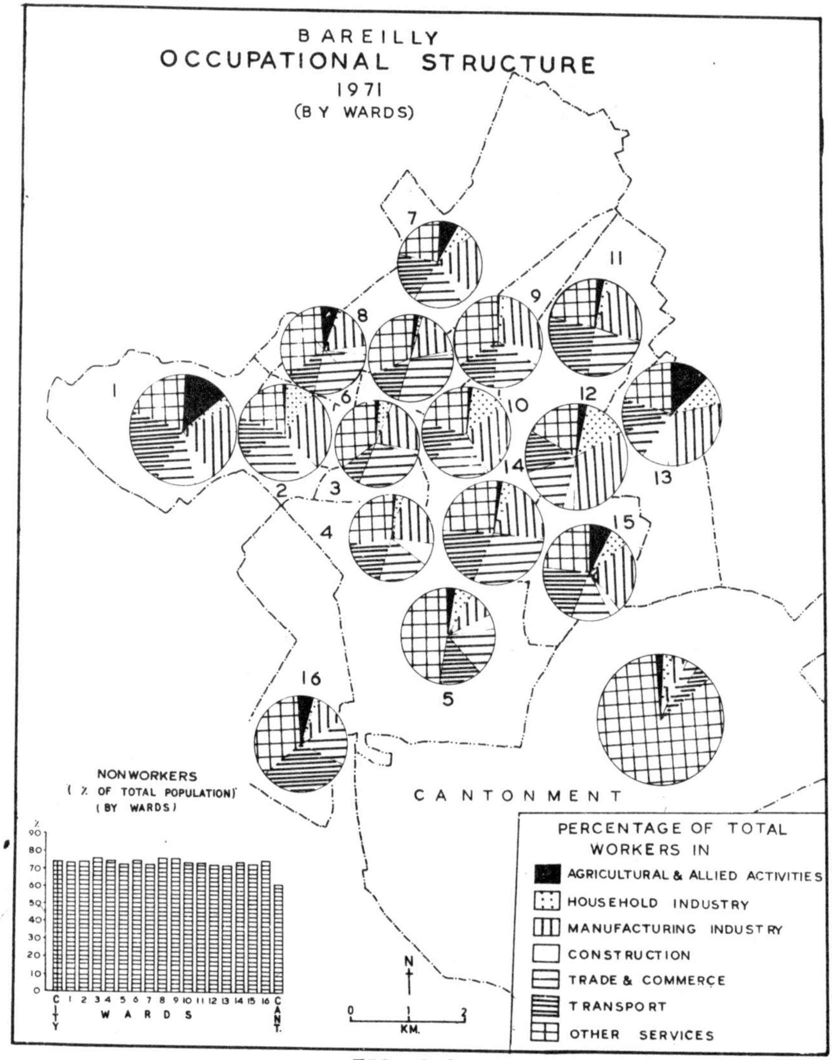

FIG. 3.9

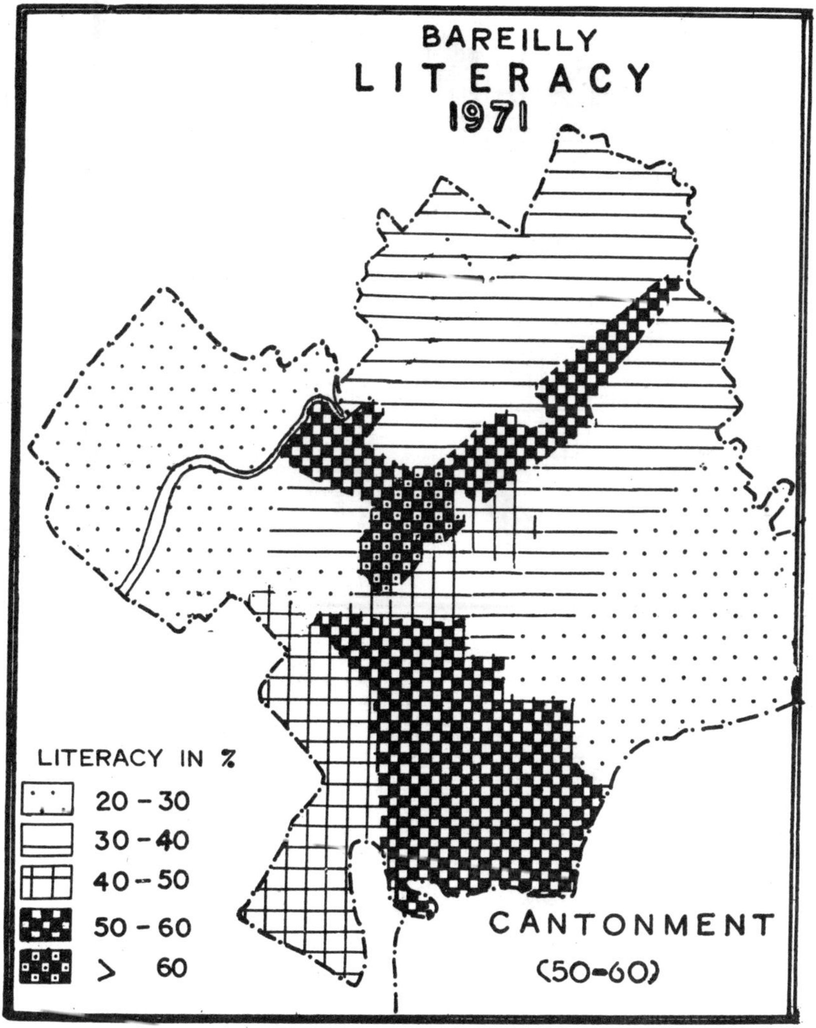
BAREILLY
LITERACY
1971
LITERACY IN %
20 - 30
30 - 40
40 - 50
50 - 60
> 60
CANTONMENT
(50-60)

FIG. 3.10

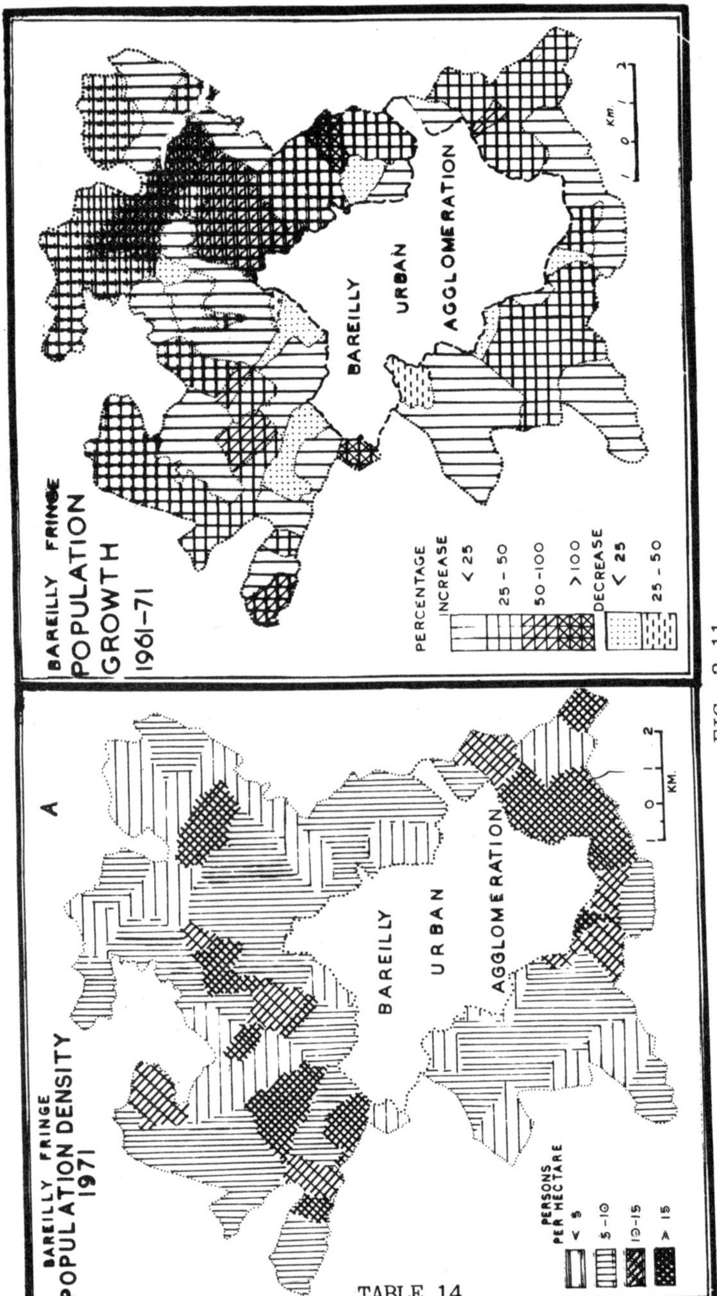
BAREILLY FRINGE
POPULATION GROWTH
1961-71
PERCENTAGE
INCREASE
< 25
25 - 50
50-100
>100
DECREASE
< 25
25 - 50
BAREILLY
URBAN
AGGLOMERATION
KM.
1 0 1 2
A
BAREILLY FRINGE
POPULATION DENSITY
1971
PERSONS PER HECTARE
< 5
5-10
10-15
> 15
BAREILLY
URBAN
AGGLOMERATION
KM.
1 0 1 2
TABLE 14

FIG. 3.11

TABLE 3.14 **Variation in Population Density by Distance Increase**

Distance in Km. from city Centre	Population Density (Persons per hectare)	
	1961	1971
2-3	6.1	5.9
3-4	5.6	6.0
4-5	5.8	7.6
5-6	6.5	9.7
6-7	8.7	12.5
7-8	6.5	8.7
8-9	5.6	7.3
9-10	-	5.3

Source : Calculated on the basis of 1961 & 1971 census data.

LITERACY : Being shadow of town more educated people reside in the urban fringe than the remote rural villages. Fig. 3.12 B indicates that in north-west a few villages of primary urban fringe representing 50 percent of more people as literates. Industrail fringe including C.B. Ganj, institutional-cum-residential fringe of north which includes I.V.R.I. and defence area, and few adjoining villages comprise 20 percent or more persons as literate. Some scattered villages in the southern part, mostly on Budaun road, indicate the same pattern. Thus literacy is not very much linked with the distance but mainly on the standard of the people who are living in those villages.

PARTICIPATION RATE : A high participation rate is often associated with a low dependency ratio and vice-versa. Participation rates are higher in most of the areas of the fringe when compared to the city itself. Average for Urban Agglomeration is 26.6 percent. About 7 villages situated exactly at the limit of the city show highest participation ratc, i.e., more than 35 percent. Thus it may be clearly stated that the ratio of dependenmcy is lower in the inner fringe when compared both to the central city or the Secondary fringe.

NON-AGRICULTURAL WORKERS

The mean percentage of workers engaged in non-agricultural occupation to total workers for the fringe of Bareilly is 35 percent and for Primary urban fringe it is 62 percent. The occupational structure tends to have wide variations from village to village and a good number of people are engaged in secondary and tertiary sectors of ....fig 12

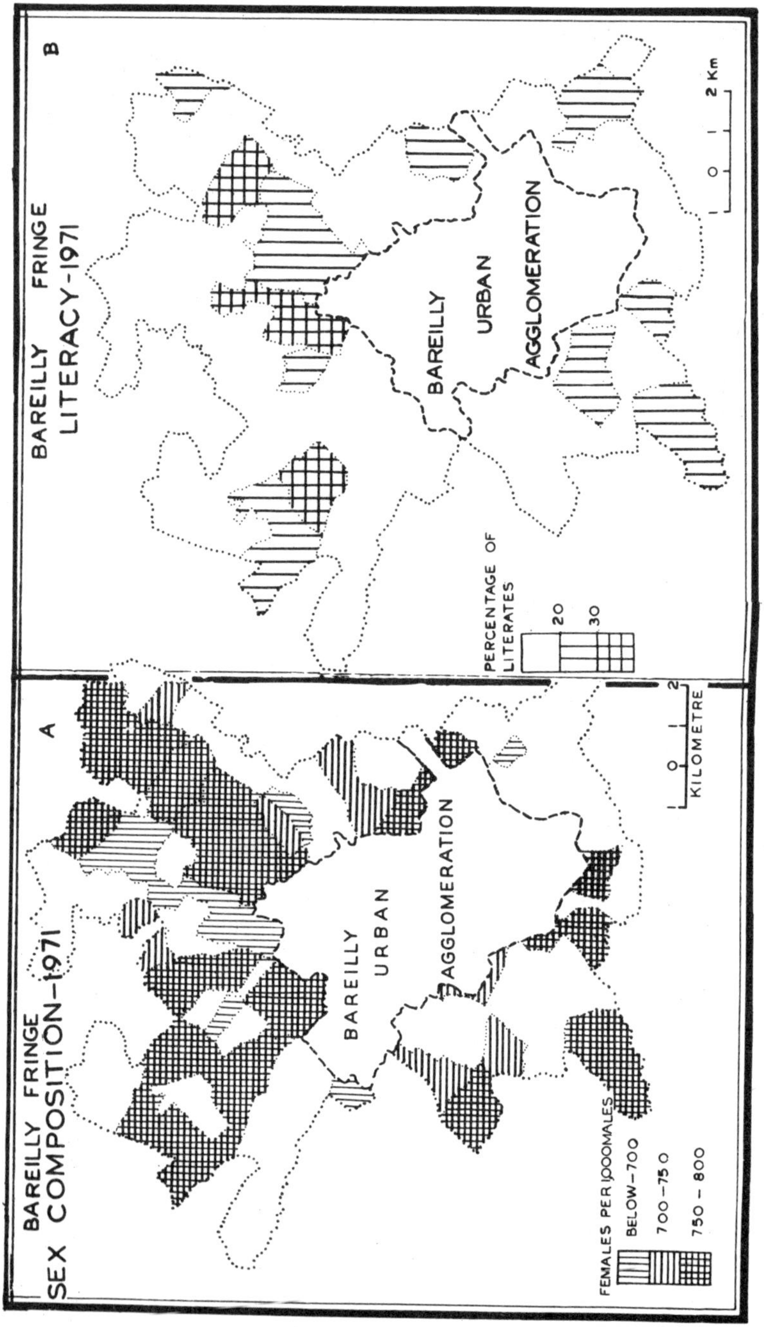
BAREILLY FRINGE
SEX COMPOSITION-1971
A
BAREILLY
URBAN
AGGLOMERATION
FEMALES PER 1,000 MALES
BELOW-700
700-750
750-800
0
1
2
KILOMETRE
BAREILLY FRINGE
LITERACY-1971
B
BAREILLY
URBAN
AGGLOMERATION
PERCENTAGE OF LITERATES
20
30
0
1
2 Km

FIG. 3.12

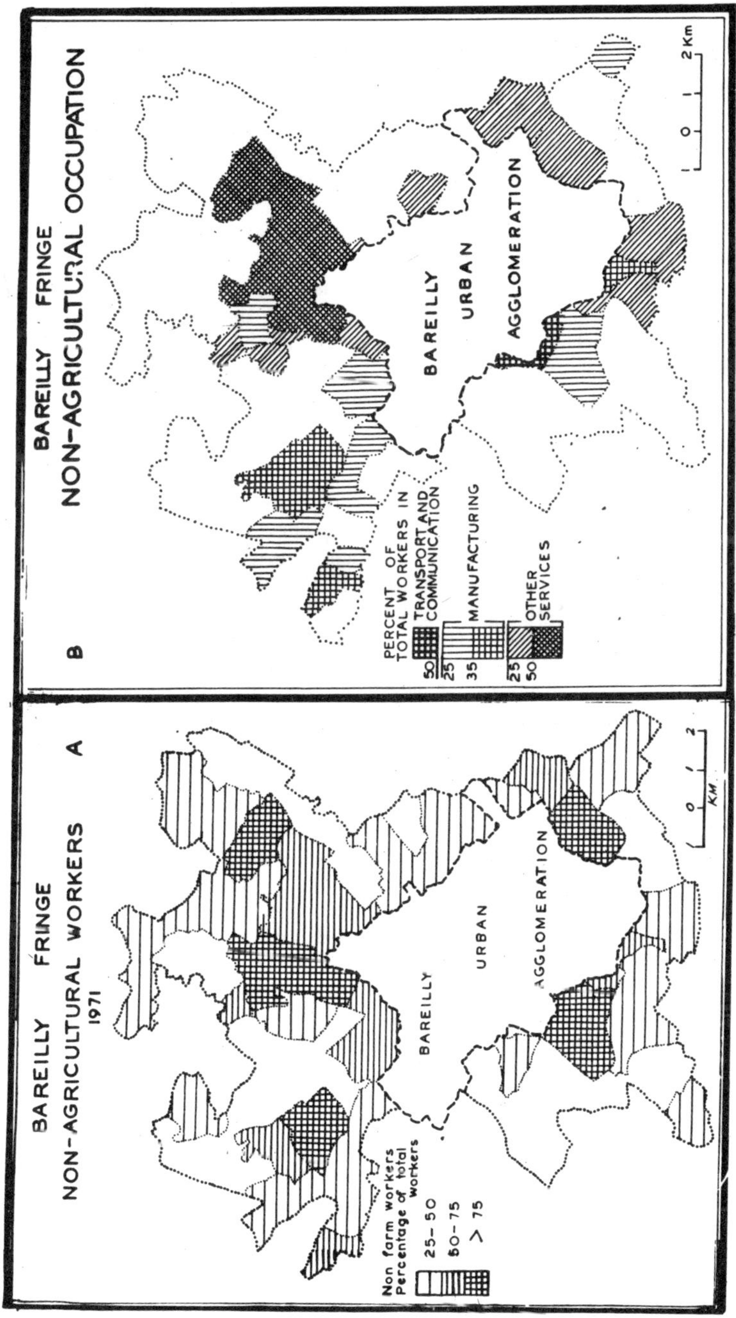
BAREILLY FRINGE
NON-AGRICULTURAL WORKERS
1971
A
Non farm workers
Percentage of total workers
25–50
50–75
> 75
BAREILLY
URBAN
AGGLOMERATION
0 1 2
KM
B
BAREILLY FRINGE
NON-AGRICULTURAL OCCUPATION
PERCENT OF TOTAL WORKERS IN
50
TRANSPORT AND COMMUNICATION
25
35
MANUFACTURING
25
50
OTHER SERVICES
BAREILLY
URBAN
AGGLOMERATION
0 1 2 Km

FIG. 3.13

economic activity. Fig. 3.13 A shows that in the villages near the city and along the road and railway lines, percentage of non-agriculutral workers in the toral workers is more than 50. Almost all the workers of Khalilpur (96%), Faridpur Choudhary (90%), Udaipur Khas (99%), Nagaria Parixit (89%) and Nekpur (89%) are engaed in non-agricultural activities.

The mean percentage of workers in manufacturing is 14 percent. As it is clear from (Fig. 3.13 B), most of the areas of the western fringe are dominated by workers engaged in manufacturing. Thus this part may be called the industrail fringe of Bareilly. Here three villages, namely Khalilpur (70%), Jauharpur (43%), and Chandpur Jogian (51%) are very important in this respect. Four or five neighbouring villages also show their 25 to 35 percent of working population as industrial workers.

Only one village, namely Nekpur, which has partly been included in the city, shows 52 percent of its working pouplation engaged in trade and commerce. Very few vilages, mostly situated along some roads in the Primary fringe, represent about 10 percent of their working people in this activity (See Appendix III for village level data).

The mean percentage of workers engaged in the categroy 'Other Services' is about 22, while in Primary Urban Fringe, it has been marked as 31 percent. In among 18 villages more than 25 percent workers are under this categroy.

In the study area, it appears that there has been a steady increase in the values of this variable in most of the urban villages or in Primary urban fringe areas during the last two decades. For instance, the proportion of non-agricultural work-force had incrased during 1961-71 from 92 percent to 96 percent in Khalilpur-Clutterbuckganj, 70.6 to 99 percent in Udaipur Khas, 78 to 90 percent in Faridpur Choudhary and from 48 percent to 89 percent in Nagaria Parixit. This speaks of the dynamism that these areas seem to be gaining economically.

REFERENCES

Atkinson, E.T. (Ed.) **Statistical, Descriptive and Historical Account of the N.W. Provinces of India**, Vol. V, **Rohilkhand Div.** Pt. I complied by H.C. Conybeare, Allahabad (1879).

Brian J.L. Berry, James W. Simmous, and Robert J. Tennant

(1963), "Urban Population Densitities: Structure and Change, **Geogr. Rev.** Vol. 53, pp. 389-405.

Brush, J.E. (1968) Spatial Patterns of Population in Indian Cities, **Geog. Rev.** 58, pp. 362-391.

Brush, John, E., (1973) Applications of a model to the analyss of Population Distribution in Indian cities, in R.L. Singh (Ed.). **Urban Geography in Developing Countries**, N.G.S.I., Varanasi, pp. 29-49. (References of Clark and Newlings articles are given in this paper).

Colin Clark (1951) Urban population Densities, **Jl. Royal Statist. Soc. Ser. A**, Vol. 114, pp. 460-496.

Heinrich Bleicher, Statistische Beschreibung der Stadt Frankfurt am Main and ihrer Bevolkerung (Frankfurt am Main, 1892), Population density is a negative exponential function of distance from the city centre in the equation $Dd=Do^{e\ -bd}$, Do is the population density at the centre of the city, e is the base of natural logarithms, and b, the density gradient.

Hudson, J. (1973) Density and Pattern in suburban Fringes, **Annals Ass. Ame. Geogr.**, 63, pp. 28-39.

Joshi, E.B. (1968) **U.P. District Gazetteers : Bareilly**, Lucknow, pp. 70-71.

Nevill, H.R. (1907) **Bareilly : A Gazetteer**, pp. 85, 146-147.

Lal, H. (1983) Urban Fringe of a North Indian Town: A case Study of Bareilly, **Market Studies**, vol. I, pp. 40-48.

Lal, H (1984) Population characteristics of a city and its Fringe, **Population Mapping-NATMO Calcutta.**

Lal, H. (1986) **Population Geography** (Hindi), Vasundhare Prokshan, pp. 270-278.

Martin, R.C. (1970) Sptial Distribution of Population : cities and suburbs; **Jl. of Regional Science**, 13, pp. 269-278.

Robinson A.H., J.B. Linkberg & L.M. Brinkman (1968) A correlation and Regression Analysis Applied to Rural Farm Population Densities in the Great Plains, in B.J.L. Berry & D.F. Marble (Ed.) **Spatial Analysis: A reader in Statistical Geography**, Prentice Hall, p. 295.

FOUR

Functional Land Use in the City

The study of the process of the growth of Bareilly discussed in preceeding chapters reveals that various pockets of the town have grown at different periods of time in haphazard manner without any planning. The nautre of topography together with historical, cultural economic factors and means of tranportation have played a great role in the location, character and space requirement of different urban activities within the city resulting in different types of land uses. The following table presents a broad picture of the land use types in the city.

DEVELOPED LAND

Table-1 indicates that a considerably high percentage (41.9%) of the land within municipal limits still remains undeveloped. The developed land or the builtup area in Bareilly is comparatively higher which is about 58 percent of the total municipal area. More than 53 percent of the development land or 31 percent of the total area is under residential use while industrial, commercial, recreational and administrative areas have a low percentage (less than 4%) Fig. 4.1 shows that the wards of the town lying on the periphery generally have a greater percentage (upto 50%) of undeveloped land. Most of the land under these wards is

either vacant or under agricultural use. The wards forming the cnetral core of the town have highest percentage (75 to 100%) of developed land on account of the fact that they contain most of the built-up areas of the town.

FUNCTIONAL LANDUSE

Fig. 4.2 depicts that residential land use predominates in the wards situated on both sides of Quilla, Bara Bazar,

Shahmatganj road. These wards also have greater amount of land under commercial use because most of the important commercial streets such as, Quilla, BaraBazar, Shahamtganj road, Kutubkhana, Ayubkhan crossing, College road, Shivaji marg etc. are located in these areas. Community facilities like hospitals, school and colleges, District Board office and government buildings etc. are located in Civil Lines and its neighbouring mohallas. Almost all the major units of sugar and Khandsari industry of the town are located in wards 11 and 12 which have greater share of land under industrial category. Thus based on the variable character of the urban land use, the following functional areas may be distinguishod in the city (Fig. 4.2):

1. Commercial land use
2. Residential Areas
3. Industrial land use
4. Administrative areas
5. Educational Insitutions

TABLE 4.1 **Existing Landuse break-up of Bareilly city**

Land use types		Area in hectare	% of the total developed area	% of the total area of the city
A. Developed Area		1373.4	100.0	58.1
(i)	Residential	732.1	53.3	31.0
(ii)	Commercial	58.6	4.3	2.5
(iii)	Industrial	53.9	3.9	2.3
(vi)	Govt. Offices (excluding those under Public Facilities)	65.6	4.8	2.8
(v)	Recreational playgrounds	42.5	3.1	1.8
(vi)	Public Utilities and services	7.5	0.5	0.3
(vii)	Transport	103.6	7.5	4.4
(viii)	Public and Semi-public facilities	213.8	15.6	9.0
(ix)	Major roads	95.8	7.0	4.0
B. Undeveloped area		988.9	100.0	41.9
(i)	Agriculture	605.7	70.4	20.5
(ii)	Vacant	206.9	20.9	8.8
(iii)	Water bodies	86.4	8.7	3.6
	Total	2362.3	100	100

Source : Based on the survey conducted by Town and Country Planning Dept. During the year 1969-71 and author's personal observation and field-work during 1974-75.

COMMERCIAL LAND USE

The area covered by the commercial establishments in Bareilly is 58.6 hectares which constitute 4.3 percent of the developed land and only 2.5 percent of toal area of the city. Major part of this area is occupied by the wholesale business as shown in the following table:

TABLE 4.2 **Commercial Land Use break-up**

Uses	Percentage of total Commercial Area
Food and Food Products	16.4
Soft and hard goods	
Shops etc.	20.3
Business Offices	10.9
Hotel and Hostels	4.2
Entertainment places	2.0
Wholesale markets and Warehousing	39.2
Service uses and Petrol Pumps	7.0

Source : Land use survey by T.C. & P. Dept Bareilly 1969-71.

Bareilly city, of the biggest business centres of the Upper Ganga Plain North after the State capital Lucknow, thanks to its geographical location, commands an extensive trade area. It serves as an important service centre for the rich agricultural region of the Tarai area and the forest products of the hilly areas in the north. The town has, therefore, developed as an important wholesale trading centre. The city centre, naturally is full of commerical activities from which business decreases in importance towards its periphery. The narrowing down of business activities from the thickly continuous built-up area in the centre to isolated patches towards the margins, is illustrated by Fig.4.3. Here, on business streets, beaded along lines of traffic shopping nucleation of varying grades have emerged.

CENTRAL BUSINESS DISTRICT

The central business district (CBD) is the core of the city. Shahmatganj-Barabazar-Quilla road is the central nerve of business and commerce of Bareilly town. General business establishments, wholesale mandies, financing and credit organizations, specialized business establishments flourishing on the local house-holds and cottage industries for which Bareilly is famous, such as, zari work, surma products, wood craft, tyresole shoe etc. are dispersed along this road. This runs almost in the midest of the present built-up area in an east-west direction dividing the town into two parts i.e. in the north and south.

The general business of the town is chiefly localized at the crossing of Junction-Nainital roads near Kutubkhana. Main business concentration extends upto rail-road level crossing near Quilla in the west over a distance of about 2 Km. and in the east upto Shahmatganj about a Kilometer of distance from this intersection. The area nearby this crossing may be termed as Central Business District of Bareilly. This narrow road of 6 to 8 metre width is one of the busiest, oldest and well maintained roads of the town and is flanked on either side by a continuos line of two storeyed shops.

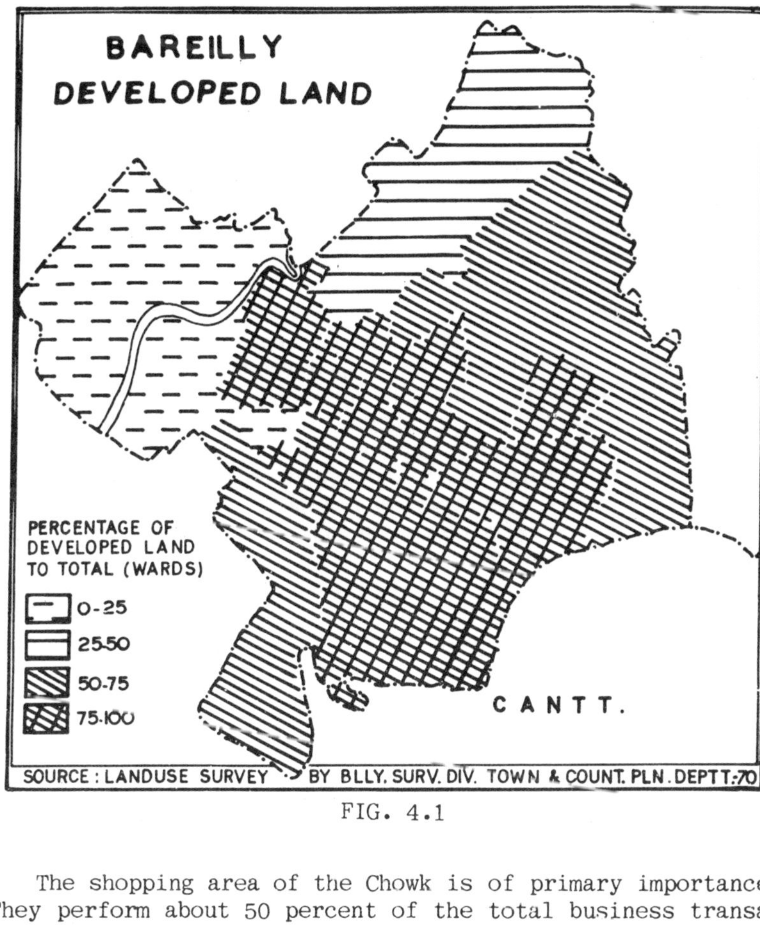

FIG. 4.1

The shopping area of the Chowk is of primary importance. They perform about 50 percent of the total business transations. General merchandise, clothing, furniture, stationery, drug and chemicals and household goods as well as banks and commercial agencies dominate the retail services in this area. Surma (eye's powder) shops appear more frequently here. The western part of this business area known as Bara Bazar, possess numerous wholesale and retail cloth shops, dispensaries, book stalls, brassware and jewellery shops. Further west towards Quilla side there is a grain mandi and several shops of daily needs.

On the east of the Town Hall at Shahmatganj road extends the biggest trade and commerical centres of the city. Retail shops of iron and metal goods, mill stores, crockery, shoes, bangles etc. are often seen. The other road connecting Alamgirganj have shops of spices, paints, jewellery, unani dispensaries etc.

Towards north, on Koharapeer road are located shops for chemist, perfumeries, furniture, bicycles, motor part dealers, engineering workshops, sweets, grain and vegetable shops and a number of other.

In the southern part of the town on junction road, or now know as Motilal Nehru Road, a new refugee market, namely Punjabi Market has been established with newly built 164 shops on the ground of Govt. High School during 1950-52. Here, two other organized shopping areas, such as, Subash Market and Pant Market have developed recently and this complex has become the busiest new centre of the town (Fig.4.4). Most of the offices, schools, Roadways bus stands, hospitals, banks, cinemas, hostels, restaurants, sweet-shops, furnitures work shops and petrol pumps are located on this road. Similarly on Chaupala road and adjoining areas are located wholesale betal shops, chemists and drugist and furhter away in Kishore market there are distillery, tailors, sweet sellers and shops of furniture, electrical goods and daily consumptions. It is followed by a large number of foot-path vendors dealing with numerous cheap articles of daily uses.

The shopping area has further extended on the narrow alleys meeting these roads at various points. A few important streets are Gali Arya Samaj, near Bara Bazar crossing, Gali Maniharan in the east of Bara Bazar crossing on Shahmatganj road.

BAREILLY
FUNCTIONAL LAND-USE:1971

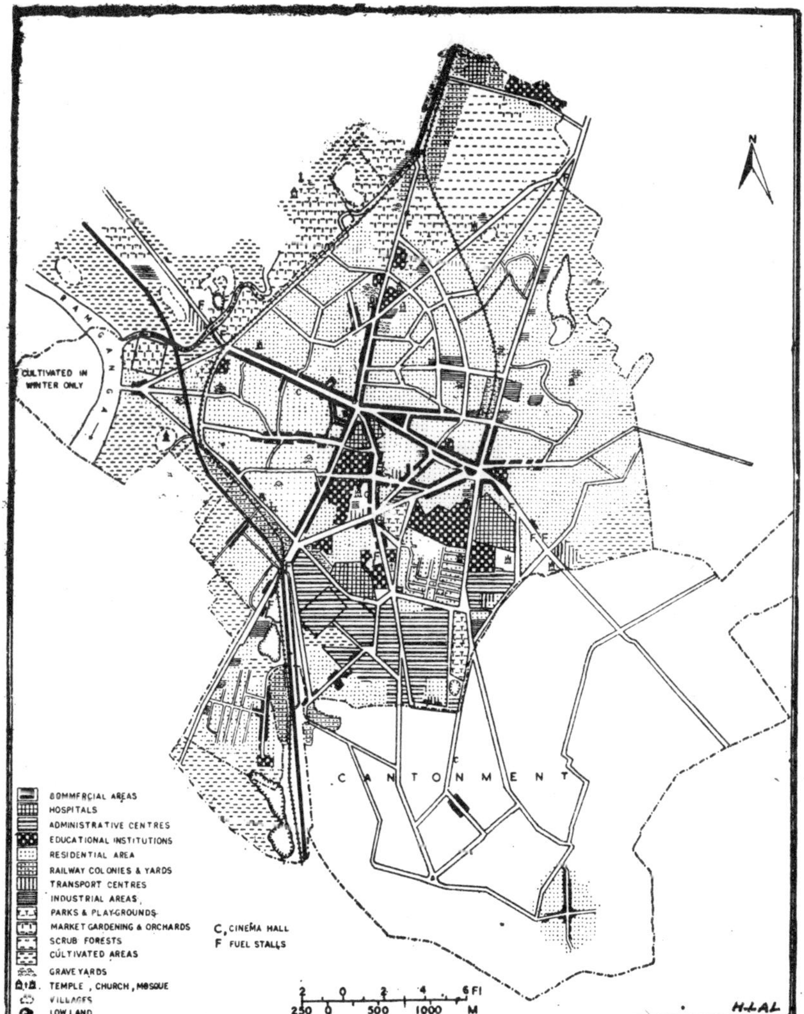

FIG. 4.2

WHOLE SALE SHOPPING AREAS

THE GRAIN MARKETS:

The city of Bareilly is the main distributing centre for the markets of the district as well as the region and the main commodities marketed in these mandies are oil seeds, wheat, jaggery, pulses and paddy.

Grain markets which require much space for godowns loading and unloading and packing, occupy several enclosures in the outer zone where land values are lower. Further, these areas are the entry points for the town through Lucknow-Bareilly-Meerut national highway from east and west respectively.

THE BAMBOO AND TIMBER MARKETS:

These markets are located on Shahmatganj road further west in between chowk and grain mandi. Some wholesale timber establishments are found on Pilibhit road near Shahmatganj railway station. These areas have the advantage of colleecting forest timber and bamboo by trucks and goods-trains from nearby Tarai forest and meet the local demand

FURNITURES SHOPS:

Bareilly is well known for its wooden and steel furnitures. The wholesale and exporting trade of furniture is largely carried on through individual firms and factory owners. Government itself is an enterpriser of the manufactured articles from the Central Wood-Work Institute, Bareilly. As the factories are normally located mixed with residential houses, the commercial frims dealing with wholesale business are also present in every nook and corner of the town. Thus, there is no wholesale shopping areas dealing exclusively in furniture. However, major establishments dealing with this trade are located at Ayubkhana crossing, Saraikhan and Kalibari area. Retail trade in furniture is carried out in almost every street of the city.

OTHER MARKETS:

Another product of importance among wholesale commercial goods are durries, cane products and surma. Surma shops acquiring less space are centred in the inner market along roads at Kutubkhana and nearby Barabazar; while cane products and durri are marketed in the eastern middle zone of the town. Similarly wholesale shopping of tobacco has developed in the old town. There are 52 godowns for storage and pounding of dried tobacco. The wholesale market of Khandsari is located in its manufacturing area, that is, in Shahdana and Quilla.

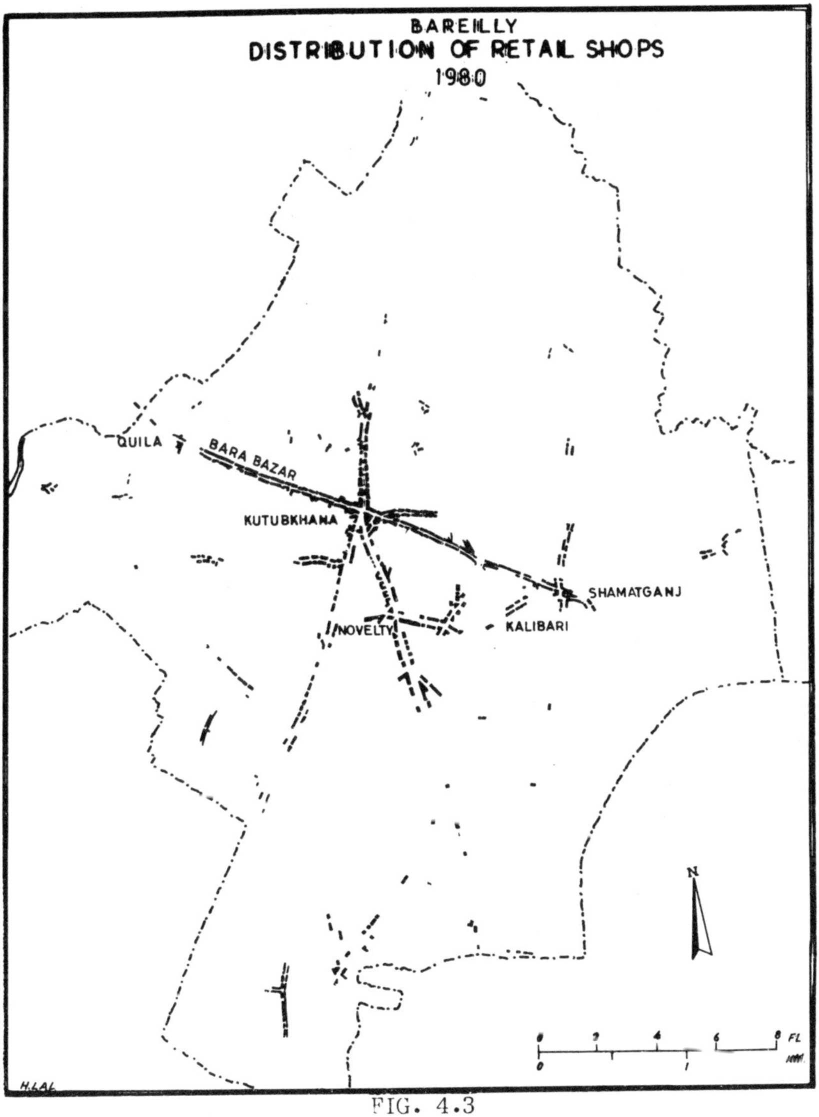

FIG. 4.3

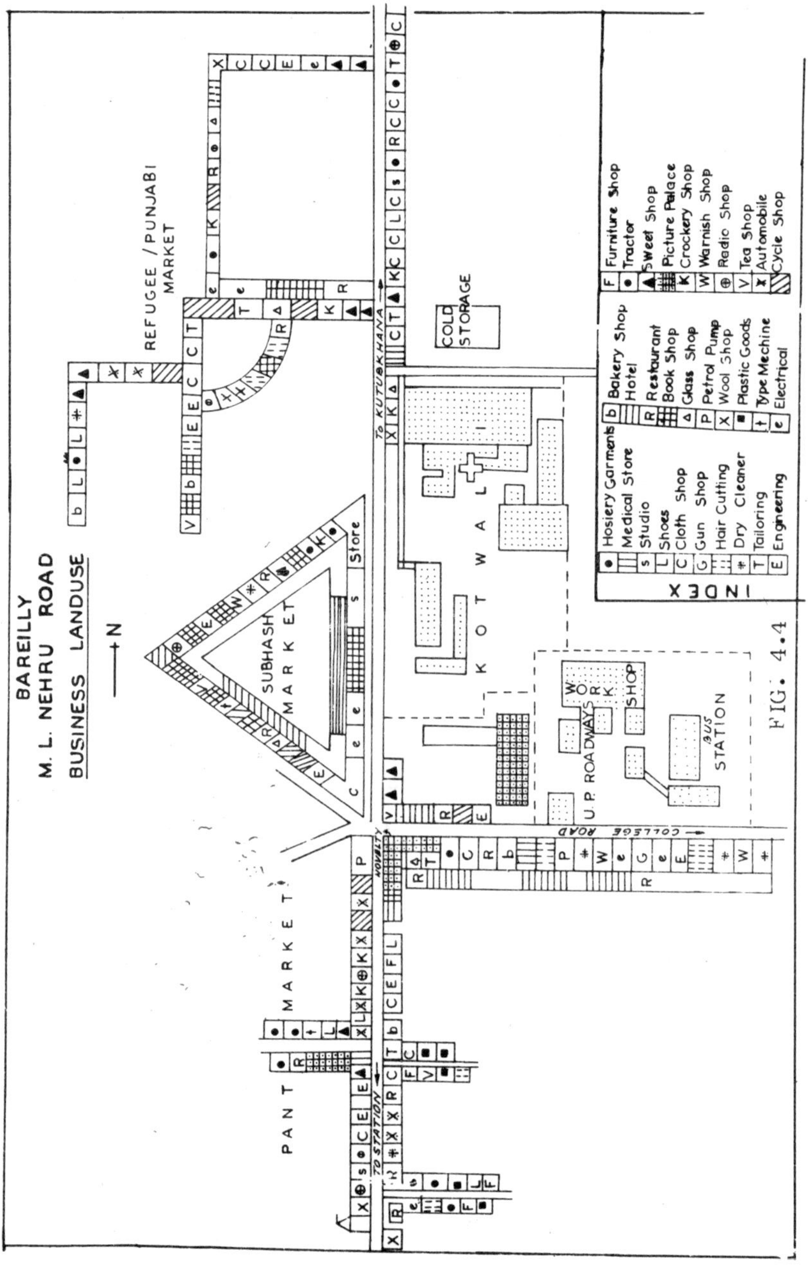
BAREILLY
M. L. NEHRU ROAD
BUSINESS LANDUSE
N
REFUGEE / PUNJABI MARKET
SUBHASH MARKET
PANT MARKET
KOTWALI
COLD STORAGE
U.P. ROADWAYS WORK SHOP
BUS STATION
To KUTUBKHANA
TO STATION
COLLEGE ROAD
NOVELTY
Store
INDEX
Hosiery Garments
Medical Store
Studio
Shoes
Cloth Shop
Gun Shop
Hair Cutting
Dry Cleaner
Tailoring
Engineering
Bakery Shop
Hotel
Restaurant
Book Shop
Glass Shop
Petrol Pump
Wool Shop
Plastic Goods
Type Mechine
Electrical
Furniture Shop
Tractor
Sweet Shop
Picture Palace
Crockery Shop
Warnish Shop
Radio Shop
Tea Shop
Automobile
Cycle Shop

FIG. 4.4

VEGETABLES AND FRUIT MARKETS:

Accessibility, plenty of space and seclusion are the chief factors responsible for the location of such markets. Hence, the vegetables markets are situated along the main roads on the periphery of the city in the west as well east. There are three vegetables and fruit markets situated on the main commercial street. First one is the west at Quilla, second at Kutubkhana in the middle and the third at Shahmatganj forming the eastern end. The Quilla market is well connected by vegetable producing areas as well as the city railway station where fruits and vegetables are being brought from different parts of the district as well as neighbouring areas. Early in the morning this place becomes crowded with a large number of buyers and sellers. A meat and fish market is also situated in this market in a separate enclosure.

The fruit-cum-vegetable market of Kutubkhana is located in the heart of the city. This is the old main Subzi Mandi of the city and caters to the needs of the majority of inner urban population. Shahmatganj vegetable market situated in the east, coveres a large area.

MARKETS FOR HEAVY AND BULKY MATERIALS:

The wholesale market for heavy goods like machine tools, implements, automobiles, scooter-cycles etc. requiring more space has developed in Civil Lines and Cantonment. These shopping areas are occupying peripheral position outside the inner zone and near the railway station mainly due to the reason that these materials are generally brought from the othrer towns either by train or by trucks.

Hides and skins are the other wholesale commercial goods whose raw material is imported from Nainital, Almora and Ranikhet. Alamgiriganj lying in the old eastern part is the main centre of distribution asd most of the tanners, generally mohammdans, reside in this area for generation.

RESIDENTIAL AREA

Land under residential area forms a major use of the total urban land in Bareilly. About 53 percent (732 hectare) of the total developed land is under this category. The present pattern of residential land use shows a mixed character of both planned and unplanned growth in the city. Like other cities of the state the heart of the inner zone is highly congested. The peripheral areas including Civil Lines, have very low density of houses. Existing physical features have played an important role in influenceing the pattern of residential areas.

UNPLANNED RESIDENTIAL DEVELOPMENT

INNER ZONE OR RESIDENTIAL-CUM-COMMERICAL AREA:

The residential area of inner zone did not grow on according to pre-conceived plan. They are the oldest settled parts of the town retaining the narrow zig-zag pattern of streets, typical of any old town of India. The Barabazar-Shahmatganj road, the nerve of the major business activities of the town, provides diversified economic opporetunities attracting larger number of population. The Bisalpur road, chaupala road and Alamgirganj road are the other principal commercial streets of the inner zone inviting heavy concentration of population. The wards falling within this zone, such as ward No.3, has the highest density of about 63 houses per hectare. Other wards of the area have also high density ranging from 45 to 60 houses per hectare.

In addition to the commercial activity, some distinct cultural barriers like railway tracks in the south-west, the Civil Lines and defence area in the south have restricted the growht of this residential zone in those directions. Further, the low land stretching in south-west direction, liable to inundation by the river Ramganga has provided little opportunity for the extention of the residential area.

The area is thus fully built-up and there is serious dearth of open spaces. The roads and streets are extremely narrow , dark and dingy. Electric and telephone poles, open drains running along the streets and the projections of the high buildings with no set-backs, further aggravate the situation by narrowing down the width of the streets. Further, these streets are usually interspersed with small open squares having a well, a religions place of worship along one or more shady trees. These areas, especially north-western part of this inner zone, are generally constitute the low-lying areas of the town with poor or no drainage and witness scenes of serious flooding during rains. In fact the conditions of living are far from satisfactory and the whole of this area has been designated as slums requiring iediate renewal schemes.

RESIDENTIAL LOCALITIES ACROSS THE RAILWAY TRACK

A number of residential localities have grown during sixtees of the present century across railway tracks in the south-west and west direction of the city. Nearness to the place of work, educational institutions and other public amenities have favoured their location in this part. Important among them is Subash Nagar which has grown in the south west of the city in between Budaun road and Northern Railway track in Nekpur mauja in 1954. As the area is adjacent to N.R. Junction station, the railways have constructed residential quarters for their employees in Subash Nagar. Its situation near the Civil Lines have also encouraged its employees to find residentail accomodation in this locality. Location of Sugar factory and some other newly constructed small manufacturing units in this direction have also given impetus to house building activities in this area.

A general retail market, food-grain and vegetable market have also developed in Subhash Nagar to cater the needs of the locality and the adjoining areas of Civil Lines, Malgodam road, Nekpur and the nearby villages.

The greatest draw-back of this locality is that it is not properly linked with the main city. Gurudwara road, the nly link, runs through an underpass of inadequate width and is often inundated durign rains creating an acute problem for vehicular traffic and padestrians. The other link through Budaun road is a longer one but the traffic is often obstructed due to level crossing. The two overhead bridges constructed by the railways is only fr the use of padestrians. Bounded by the railway track on one side and the low lying areas liable to flood on the other, this locality has developed on a limited space in a haphazard manner.

Madhinath is another important locality which has developed in the west of the ity across the railway track. This locality shows the sign of planned development in the form of straight and reular street pattern. But the actual physical development has not taken place according to some planning standard.With a coverage of over a square kilometer, the width of road and streets are narrow with the building lines coming right on to the street edges making the street dark and dingy. Some government offices have been established here. A small market has also grown in Madhinath. With a view to solving the problem of traffic jam at level crossing an overhead-cum-underpass bridge for padestrians and light vehicular traffics has been constructed. Just as in the case of Subhash Nagar, the railway tracks and the low lying land liable to floods and water logging have restricted the physical growth causing high density of houses and population.

SUBURBAN VILLAGES:

With the extension of Municipal limits a number of villages have also been incorporated in the urban area. The built-up area bear an imprint of the typical rural character of unplanned growth with high population density. The villages included are Surkha, Salehnagar, Newada Seikhan etc.

PLANNED RESIDENTIAL AREAS

In addition to the Civil Lines, a few planned residential colonies have also been developed either by the private individuals or by the government.

THE CIVIL LINES

Of all the areas developed according to plan, Civil Lines has the largest area occupying about 17 percent of the total urban area. This area was origionally developed by Britishers who carved out extensive land for the construction of spacious bunglows. This has, therefore, grown at an extremely low density of about 30-40 persons per hectare. The roads are straight and wider. Situated between heavily congested older city in the north and the Cantonment area in the south, the Civil lines found an ample opportunity for the development of the major facilities and work centres of the city within the area. Unfortunately their concentration at one place has given rise to many problems which the town is facing at present. On account of the high remunerative land values, the residential quarters with large open spaces are either being sub-divided into smaller independent plots or are being let out for multifacious uses. Often the frontage of old and new residences are being converted for commercial, industrial and other more lucrative non-residential uses. Among such colonies developed within Civil Lines are Rampur Garden Coloney, Hydel Coloney, state official residences near the court and Gandhi park etc.

RAMPUR GARDEN COLONEY:

Officially known as Murtaza Colony, it came into existence in 1956 and is one of the best residential localities of the city. It has been developed with modern type of houses along wide straight roads (Fig.4.5). The colony consists of a school, parks, a shopping centre with departmental stores, a welfare centre and a picture palace has recently been erected to cater for the need of the people of this posh area. Most of the bunglows of this area belong to big businessman, doctors, lawyers and high ranked officials including engineers.

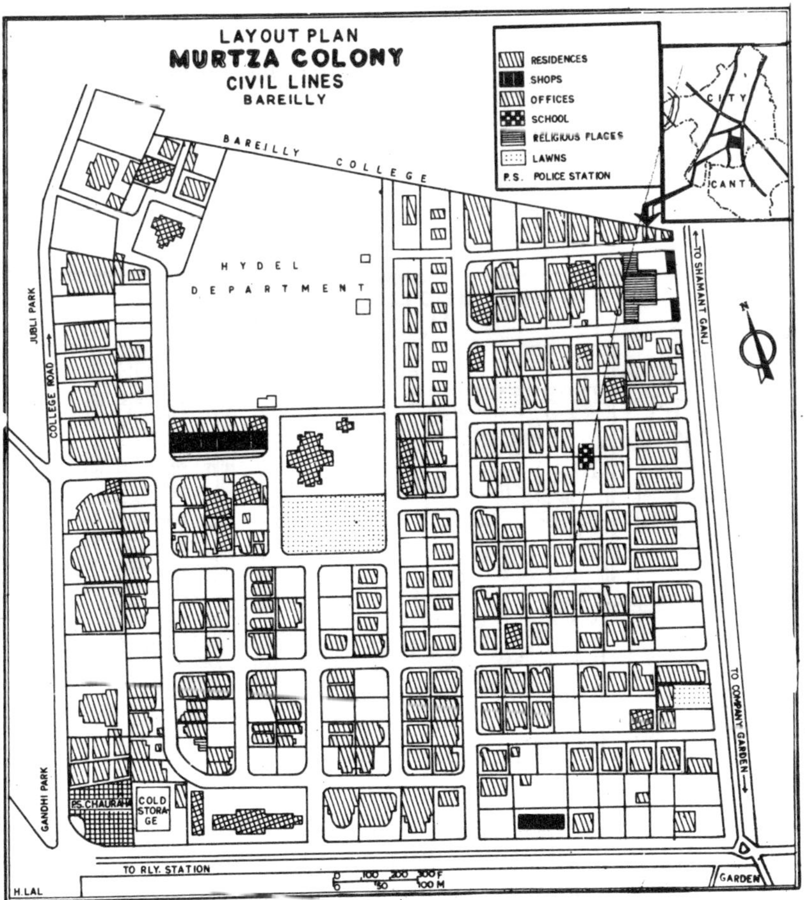

FIG. 4.5

Claraswain hospital and Church complex have also some planned residential quarters in the Civil Lines west.

Other important planned residential areas of the city are Model Town Refugee Coloney, Shahdana, Prem Nagar and Railway Colonies. The Model Town came into existence in 1952 in which 450 families are residing in 200 houses. Another refugee colony developed at Shahmatganj in 1959 to settle the refugee from west Pakistan. About 300 families are living in 125 houses. The houses are ordinary flat type modern houses. The Harijans and Social Welfare Department, U.P. has constructed a colony for Harijans in the city where about 250 such families reside.

Both Northern and North-Eastern Railways have their respective residential colonies near all the four railway stations of the city. Largetst among them is Model Coloney of Izatnagar with total number of 534 quarters housing about 2250 persons (Fig. 4.6). Provisions of shops, school and playground and parks have been made accordingly.

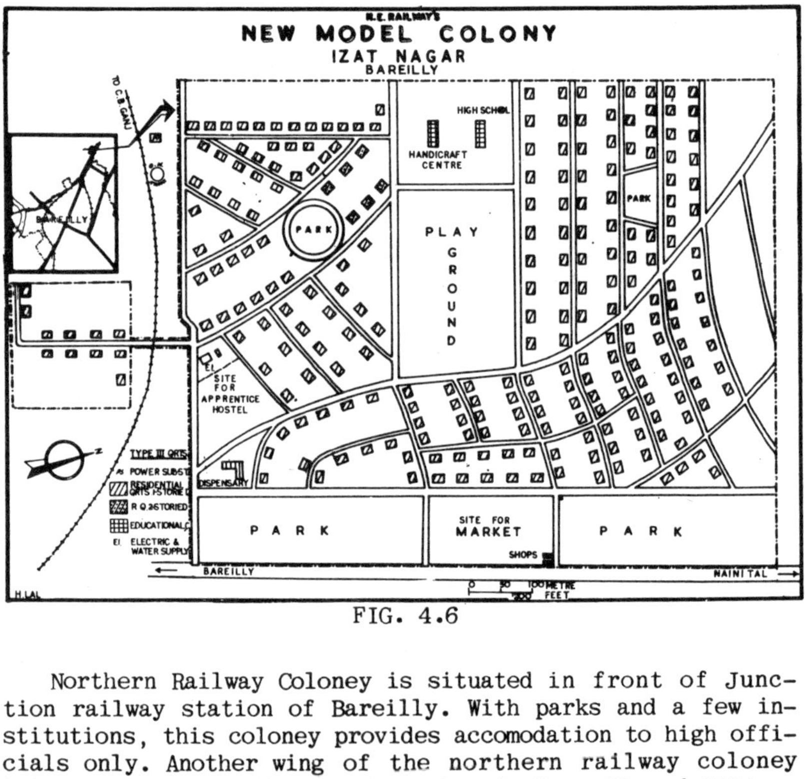

FIG. 4.6

Northern Railway Coloney is situated in front of Junction railway station of Bareilly. With parks and a few institutions, this coloney provides accomodation to high officials only. Another wing of the northern railway coloney lying just behind the station, is of class II and IIItype residences and consists of 735 houses in which about 3500 railway employees are living.

INDUSTRIAL LAND USE

There is no planned development of industrial sectors within municipal limits. The industrial units established within congested resisdential and commercial areas are functioning at the cost of the health and hygeine of the inhabitants. The industrial establishment sites in terms of coverage, accessibility, loading unloading and packing facilities etc. are so packed that there is not room for futher expansion. The high land and rental value in the inner zone have permitted the establishment of only small scale industries, such as Khandsari, furniture, cane etc.in this area. On the other hand, the heavy or extensive industrial units are generally situated in the outer zone. Noted among them are H.R. Sugar Factory, at Nekpur and Koedesia Engineering works near Izatnagar. However, the small scale industries are scattered throughout the city-proper with its maximum concentration in the Nai Basti area which is famous for its 'Khandsari' (raw sugar) industry (Fig.4.2).

The total area covered by the industrial establishment, both large and small, is 54 hectares which constitutes 3.9 percent of the total area of the city. Out of this area 68.2 percent is occupied by light industries as shown in the following table:

TABLE 4.3 **Industrial Land-use**

Industrial Category	Percent of total Industrial Area
Light Industries	68.2
Service Industries	12.5
Extensive and Extractive Industries	9.9
Noxious Industries	9.4

Source : Town and Country Planning Survey, Bareilly.

During the third five year plan period, under the scheme of establishing workshops with facilities of motive power, water storage, office accomodation etc. for small industries, the State Government encourage the development of industries in the district. Under this scheme a medium size industrial estate is being established at C.B.Ganj, in an area of 6.8 hectare. 15 workshops having been constructed in the first phase. Administratively it is controlled by the

State Directorate of Industries. The Second, industrial area is being developed by U.P. State industrial Corporation Ltd on about 150 hectare of land acquired along Rampur road for this purpose.

On account of non-availability of land, enhanced municipal taxes, fees etc. and restriction on the use of land in the city, a number of heavy industries have developed in the fringe of the city in C.B. Gangj and Izatnagar in various pockets where infra-structure of industrial growth are available. Such industrial developments are taking place in a ribbon shape along Rampur and Nainital Roads. Majority of industries functioning at Bareilly are agro-based as well as forest based because of its settign in a rich agricultural region and Tarai forest.

Sugar industry is the only large scale industries functioning in the town. The H.R. Sugar Factory located along Badaun road at Nekpur established in 1932, employes 1000 persons during crushing seasons.

Among the importnat small scale industries, generally located in Bareilly city are the Khandsari, furniture, engineering and food products. The Bareilly areas was one of the pioneers in the manufacture of Khandsari sugar, and the industry, though seasonal, is the largest in the district even today. About 38 Khandsari units, where the sugar is produced and the by-product rab (molasses) stored , are scattered all over the town and are to a great extent responsible for the airpollution in the neighbouring area.

The city is famous for its furniture industry not only in this state but in the entire country. The furniture is of the modern type, simple in design and is usually made of Shisham wood. The first workshop of the district was satarted in 1891. The industry made rapid progress and now occupies an important place in the economy of the city. Most of the area of the city lying east of Kutubkhana is under residential-cum-industrial use and the most important industries of the area are Khandsari and furniture.

There are 12 units including Kudesia Eng. Works engaged in the engineering industry which manufacture cane crushers, iron utensils, automobile parts and various other agricultural implements. Seven mills scattered in the city produce Maida, Atta, and pulses. Bakery products, oil pressing, soap making, cutch, ice etc. are also processed in several small scale units.

ADMINISTRATIVE AREAS

The total area covered by the government offices is65.6 hectares constituting 4.8 percent of the total developed land. Out of the total area occupied by the administrative offices 81 percent covered by the State Govt. offices. Most of the zonal, regional and divisional headquarters of different central and state government departments are situated in Bareilly due to its being administrative headquarters of Rohilkhand Division.

According to their functional activities all the administrative centres may be grouped as follows: (i) State Administrative offices, (ii) Municipal Corporation office, (iii) District Courts and Sub-divisional offices, (iv) police Lines and (v) Other Government buildings.

STATE ADMINISTRATIVE OFFICES

Almost all the important State offices are situated in the southern part of the city in Civil Lines, (Fig.4.2). These office buildings are scattered over here and almost all important offices, Revenue offices and many others are housed within this region and were particularly near and around Rampur Garden area. Regional Employment Exchange Office and labour Commissioners's office etc. are also located in the south western corner of the Civil Lines.

MUNICIPAL OFFICES:

The Municipal Corporation offices dealing with administration occupy a place north of the State administration zone in between Bareilly college and Eye Hospital. It is extended in a triangular campus and town hall building is also located in the same complex.

DISTRICT COURTS:

Bareilly District Court is situated at the peripheral site of Civil Lines very near to JUnction railway station. Both Civil and Criminal Court buildings are standing here side by side. The district treasury office, and Bareilly Tahsil are situated along the other side of the Kutubkhana Station road.

POLICE LINES:

The Police Lines which require plenty of space for

Police barracks and parade grounds etc.,occupy a large area between District Jail and Chaupala Crossing almost very near to City Railway Station. Police Hospital and some other residential quarters are situated west of Chaupala crossing within main builtup area.

OTHER GOVERNMENT BUILDING:

Among other government buildings, Commissioner's office is located in between court and Rampur Garden near city park. A number of other important government offices, mostly belonging to the central government are situated beyond municipal limits, such as divisional headquarters of N.E. Railway and Indian Veterniary Research Institute (IVRI) in Izatnagar and Post and Telegraph, and Sales Tax offices in Cantonment.

There are all 123 government offices in the city with a total employment of about 9 thousand in 1971. The member of government offices have increased about 4 timesafter independence of the country.

RECREATIONAL LAND USE :

PARK AND PLAYGROUND

The total area developed as park and playgrounds in the city works out to be 42.5 hectares. In comparison to the total populatiopn of the city the shareof open spaces therefore, is very low. There are seven parks worth the name in the city. Out of these four are situated in the Civil Lines having an area of 12 hectares. The rest 3 parks with an area of 1.7 hectares only are distributed all over the city. This clearly indicates the sad state of affairs as far as the open space in the city is concerned.

PUBLIC AND SEMI PUBLIC FACILITIES:

Education, health and other miscellaneous facilities have been covered under this head. The total area covered by the public and semi-public facilities in Bareilly is 213.8 hectare, which constitute 15.6 percent of the total developed area. Educational institutions cover the highest land area (40.6 percent) under this land use (Table -4).

EDUCATIONAL INSTITUTIONS

A total number of 205 educational institutions of all

types occupying an area of 61.6 hectares are running in Bareilly with a total enrolment of about 50,000 students out of which 42 belong to primary standard. Threee degree colleges, viz., Bareilly Post Graduate College in Civil Lines for boys and girls, Shahy Gopinath Mahavidyalya in Bans Mandi and Arya Kanya Pathshala in Bhoor for girls provide facilties for higher education. Besides these other educational institutions located in two blocks, one in Civil Lines consisting of Govt. Intermediate College, Islamia College, D.A.V. College, Saraswati Vidyalaya, Deaf amd Dump school etc. The other important education block is situated on Kutubkhana Nainital road in the north where K.D.M. College, Gulab Rai Intermediate College, Manohar Bhushan Inter College are located (Fig. 4.2). These institutions requiring cheaper and specious land for school and hostel buildings, playgrounds etc. occupy a part of the outer zone.

TABLE 4.4 **Area Under Public Facilities**

	Facilities	Percentage of total land under facilities
1.	Educational Institutions	40.6
2.	Hospitals, Dispensaries, Police Stations and Fire Stations	25.9
3.	Cemetries and Cremation ground	16.4
4.	Historical and Religious monuments	11.8
5.	Social and Cultural Institutions	3.4
6.	Local Municipal Offices	1.9

Source : T. & C.P. Survey, Bareilly-1971.

It is unfortunate that the highly congested wards No.3,4,8,10 and 14 have no schools and colleges within their limits. The students residing in these wards are bound to move to the various educational institutions situated in Civil Lines and Kutubkhana--Nainital Roads further apart.

In 1973-74 there were 121 boys' Junior Basic schools run by the municipal board. In addition, there are 51 Junior Basic schools, 11 Senior Basic Schools all being run by the board. In the Cantonment, there are 2 Junior Basic schools for boys and one for girls with an enrolement of 650 boys and 290 girls in year 1971.

Apart from these there are seven technical institutes imparting training in various trades, especially in wood work and carpantery.

Bareilly College, started as a school, established in 1937 and is one of the most important institutions of the

Rohilkhand Plain. Built on a vast ground of about 250 hectares given by the Nawab of Rampur, this college imparts education in 13 subjects for Master's degree. The central part of the campus is devoted to teaching while eastern part consists of playground and swimming pool.etc. Students hostel is located in the south and teachers quarters along with Principal's Bunglow occupy the north-eastern corner of the college campus. A new post-graduate building and a library with suitable amenities have been addes to the college recently. The establishment of **Rohilkhand university** in 1975 has added much to the educational life of the city.

Opened in the first decade of this century the Post-Graduate College of Animal Sciences, **Indian Veterinary Research Institute (IVRI), Izatnagar** is one of the three major centres of research and education in animal husbandry problems providing valuable scientific knowledge, techniques and practical training for the conservation and development of livestocks. It covers a vast area (about 700 hectares) in the northern margin of the city. The main campus of the institute consisting of laboratory, office, store, packing houses, preparation block and grain godown covers 300 hectare of land while its farm extends on 400 hectares. Of this area about 300 hectares are under crop and about 100 hecatares are devoted to grazing. Another important work of this inswtitute is the making of serum animal fertilization. More than 60 students are enrolled for M.V.Sc. courses while 15 to 25 students are enlisted for Ph.D. courses.

Other important professional and technical institutues are the Govt. Central Wood Work Institute, the Sports Goods Centre, the I.T.I and the Govt. Polytechnic.

The Deaf and Dump school located in a house near Kotwali, and the Juvenile School of Rampur Garden Coloney, are of speical type of institutions.

HOSPITALS

Bareilly provides the genral and specialized medical facilities for a fairly wide region. There are three general hospitals, 4 restricted hospitals of Railways and Jails; a Mental hospital, the Eye hospital and the T.B. Clinic are specialized hospitals. All these cover 33.4 hectares of land, that is, about 25 percent of the total area under public and semi-public facilities.

FIVE

Pattern of Settlement and Landuse in the Fringe

We have noticed in the previous chapters that the character of land use, agricultural activities and settlement pattern of the fringe have undergone a considerable change due to the extension of the built-up area of Bareilly city beyond its geographical limit. The impact of urbanization is clearly marked in these changes. The process of changes and their effects on the cultural landscape within the fringe of the cities are of major concern to the urban geographers. Hence, in this chapter an attempt has been made to visualize the genral characteristics of settlement and land use pattern of the city's fringe as well as to analyse the functional impact of city on rural habitat.

Within the limited time and resources available it was not possible to analyse these changes and their impact in all the villages falling within the city fringe. Hence, five villages, namely, Khalilpur, Jauharpur, Kargaina, Mohanpur and Govindapur, have been selected for detailed studies with a view to presenting a picture of general character of these variants, their changes and their impacts in the wake of urbanization.

For the sake of presenting the genral characteristics, the villages are arranged according to their situations into four concentric circles drawn at one and half Kilometre's distance from the city centre. The spatial extent of the built-up area, pattern of house density and the nature of settlement dispersions have been studied in order to bring out the gradient of urban influences in relation to the distance from the city. Further, an attempt has been made to visualize the important landuse changes in the city's fringe. The study is based on the village level data available from the 1971 cencus and office records. The following tables illustrating the main characteristics of the radial sectors has been obtained by consolidating the village level indices.

TABLE 5.1 **Variations in the selected characteristics of the Fringe with the increase in distance :**

Characteristics	KMS. from the city centre 3-4.5	4.5-6	6-7.5	7.5-9	Average for the Fringe
1. Density of House Per Sq.Km.	79	121	81.5	70.3	98.8
2. Built-up area (% of total area)	12.9	17.7	12.8	7.6	15.1
3. Area occupied by a hamlet in hectare (A/H)	158	104	144	220	128
4. Inter-hamlet distance (in Metre)	1288	1116	1261	1620	1321

Source : Calculated from 1971 census data and informations collected from the office records.

Variations in the selected characteristics of the Fringe with the increase in distance:

HOUSE DENSITY

The average house density in the fringe in about 98.8 houses per sq.km. At some places density rises upto 334 and at the same time some small and isoloated villages like sherpur (15), Bhagwatipur (13) possess a very low house density (Fig.5.1). An analysis of the above table reveals that the house density gradient indicates decline from about 131 houses per sq.km. within the inner ring to 70 houses within the outermost ring. Such sharp declining trend in house density is also noticable along Rampur and Nanital roads where it drops from 284 to 60 and from 140 to 57 respectively (table 2 and Fig. 5.2A). There is a very gentle gradient of house density along Bareilly Badaun road where it ranges between 199 to 71 houses per sq.km. The flatness of the density profile along this route is mainly due to its level terrain, prevalence of rural way of life, moderate accessibility as well as lack of any industrial establishment. Along Bareilly-Rampur road house density profile falls sharply after 4.5 to 6km. distance from the city centre. It is mainly due to the exitance of industrial satellite of Clutterbuckganj in the second sector.

The relationship of relative density to distance from

the city centre is less significant than the gradient of gross density as discussed above. A few villages situated along the river show a high relative density (above 2000 houses per sq.km.) because 'dry point' settlement sites are limited in area and a good number of houses have to be built over a comparatively small space. A few villages lying very near the municipal limit also have a high relative density due to its high land value. Areas of medium relative house density are scattered by the side of these high density villages. Low density area is comparatively more extensive. Thoreis, however, no evidence from this analysis that the gradient of relative density is a function of distance from the city.

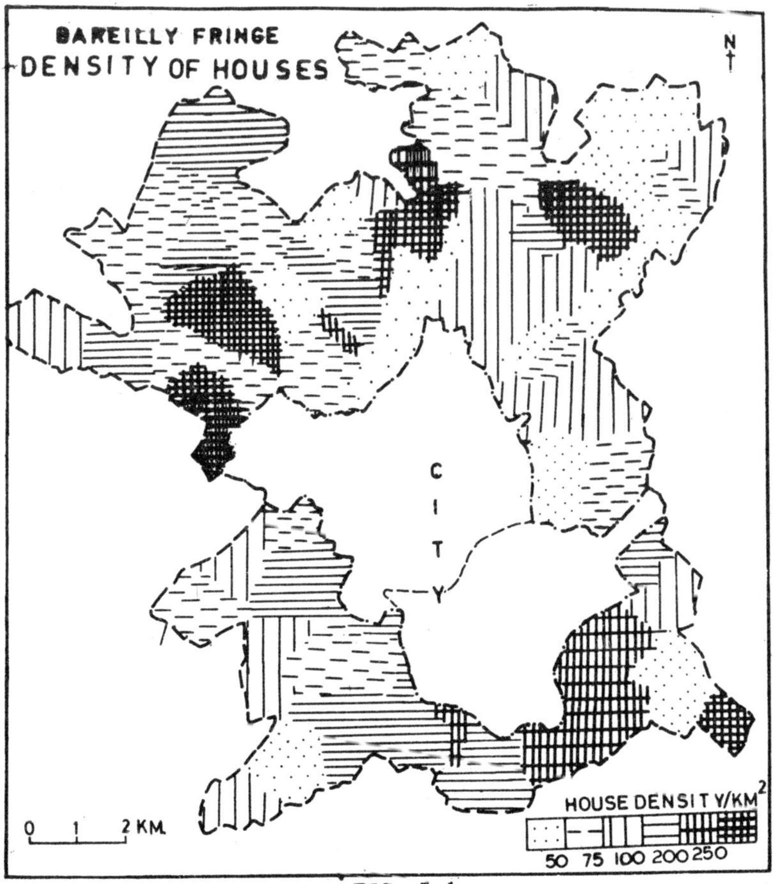

FIG. 5.1

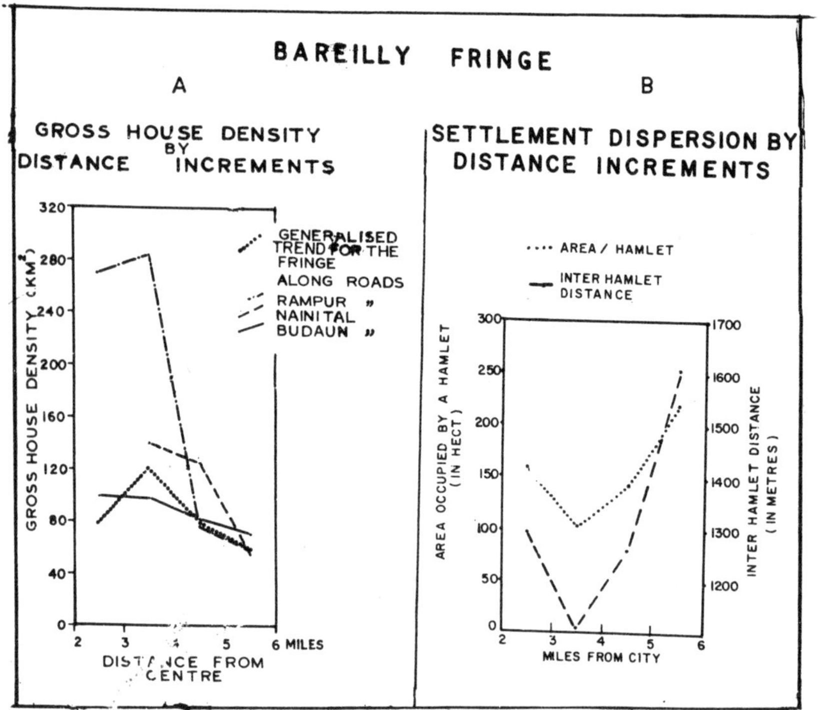

FIG. 5.2

TABLE 5.2 **Variation in house density with the increase in distance along main routes.**

Roads		Houses per Sq. Km (Km from city centre) 3-4.5	4.5-6	6-7.5	7.5-9	Average for the ribbons
Bareilly-Rampur						
	G :	270	248	76	60	175
	R :	2300	1030	415	778	1131
Bareilly-Nainital						
	G :	-	140	126	57	108
	R :	-	1589	2335	1842	3922
Bareilly-Budaun						
	G :	99	98	82	71	88
	R :	1773	1147	673	800	1089

G : General house density
R : Relative house density

Source : Computation by the author, based on census - 1971.

CHARACTER OF BUILT-AREA

One of the most noticeable impacts of urbanization upon rural landis the growth of built uo areas at the expense of agricultural land of the surrounding villages. As discussed earlier (Chapter III), the population density is maximum near the city limit and decreases outwards. In order to accommodate this population, as well as few services and activities characterised by extensive landuses, the percentages of builtup area to total area is likely to be the maximum in the inner ring. Due to this growth some patches of agricultural lands arc being eatenup by non-agricultural uses and expanding village settlements.

This trend is very clearly visible in the Fig. 5.3. Analysis of the built-up area to the total area in the study area confirms the general trend i.e.decline in the ratio of built-up area with the increase of distance from the city centre. (Table 5.3).

TABLE 5.3 **Variation in Built-up area with increasing distance**

Roads	Built up area Ratio (Kms. from City Centre)				Average for the Ribbons
	3-4.5	4.5-6	6-7.5	7.5-9	
Bareilly-Rampur	11.9	32.7	40.5	7.6	23.2
Bareilly-Nainital	-	53.5	27.1	6.6	25.7
Bareilly-Budaun	7.2	14.0	8.7	9.0	9.7

Source : Computation by the author based on office records.

Following the main thoroughfares there are three significant blocks of high ratio (above 10 percent) in this fringe. Some villages like Khalilpur (46%), Udaipur Khas (44.8%). Nagaria Parichhat (51.2%) and Faridpur Chaudhri (51.3%) may be cited as examples where maximum built-up area ratio occurs. Development of industries, industrial estates and the existance of government administrative building have played a great role in the extention of the built-up area in these localities. A narrow belt along the eastern side of the Ramganga and some inaccessible areas of the north have a very low ratio(below 5%).

Diminution of built-up area ratio with distance from the city centre is very well marked in this study area. Within a six Km. radius frm the centre of Baraiily this ratio is 17.7 percent which falls to 12.8 and 7.6 percent in the next two outer sectors. The distance-density curve makes a convex form along the Bareilly-Rampur road (with 40.5% in the third ring), steep gradient along NainitalRoad and in gentle but concave form along Budaun-Road.

BAREILLY FRINGE

BUILT-UP AREA

1971

FIG. 5.3

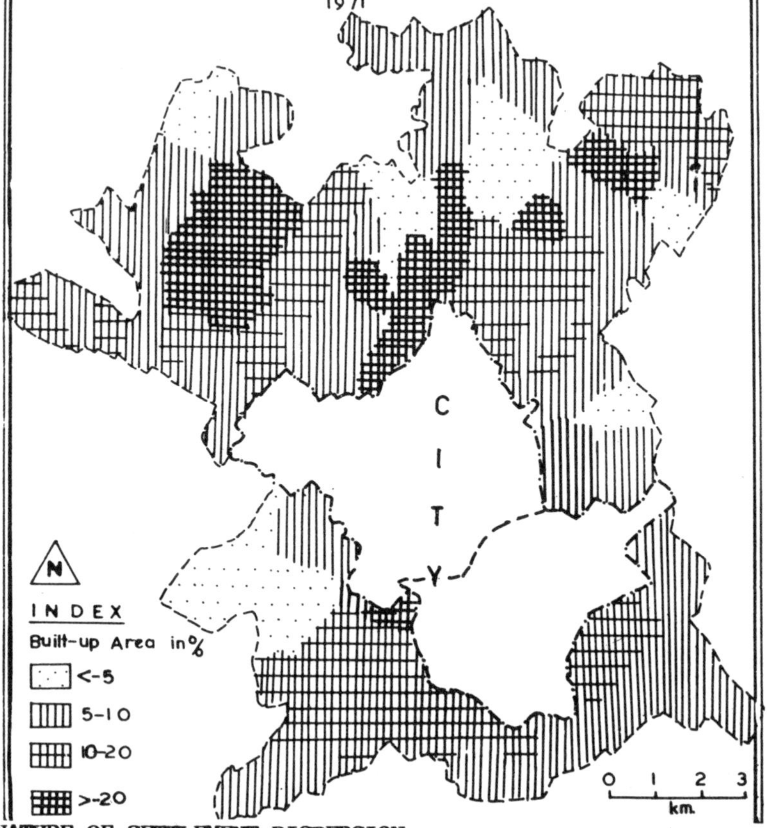

NATURE OF SETTLEMENT DISPERSION

The level fertile land of this area has provided an uniform attractive sities for human habitations. The facilities of transport and communication growth and urban influences have facilitated the growth of scatered villages, in the city's fringe.

Thus, it has brought a significant change in the general distributional aspects of the settlement. Fig. 5.4 reveals a marked variability in forms and distributional patterns of the rural settlement of the area. The western part of the fringe where adequate transport facilities exist, high frequency of settlement occur. Least accessibility and the rough terrain have restricted the growth and distribution of rural settlements in the north eastern part of the fringe. It is noteworthy that the villages adjacent to city are smaller in size and most of them are connected either by main or link roads. Comparatively large and compact villages are observed in the peripery of the fringe.

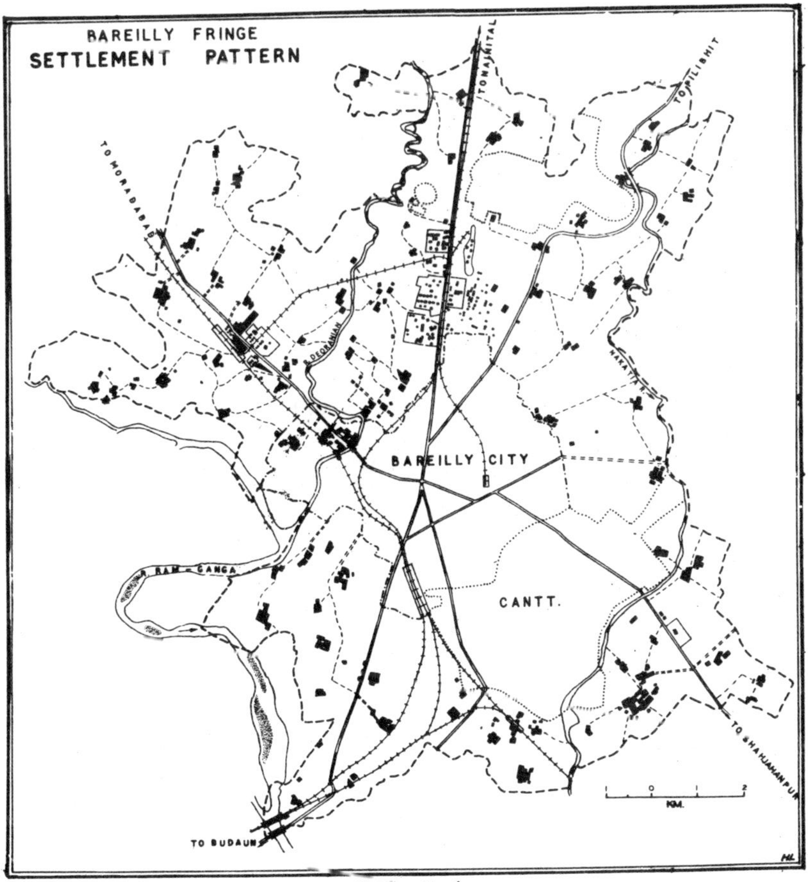

FIG. 5.4

The entire population of Bareilly fringe lives in 77 villages consisting of 103 hamlets, which gives an average unit area of 170.5 hectare for a village and 12.8 hectare for a hamlet brining in an average interhamlet distance of 1.32 km. The fig. 5.5 reveals the areal distribution of the dispersion of settlements. Most of the villages in the fringe show a fairly to very scattered nature of dispersion. 29 villages have very scattered nature of dispersion while 21 show a fairly scattered-dispersion comprising of the industrial area and the adjoining regions. 12 villages, showing medium dispersion, are located in patches all over the fringe, though mostly lying towards the south and south-west of the Cantonment. These villages have very dense concentration of houses over the residential sites. The medium dispersion is often the result of the isolated nature of settlement due to social distance between different castes of the parent villages. Rest 16 villages show a close dispersion, frequently visible over the high bank of the Ramganga. These village are small in size and the entire population is concentrated in a single hamlet.

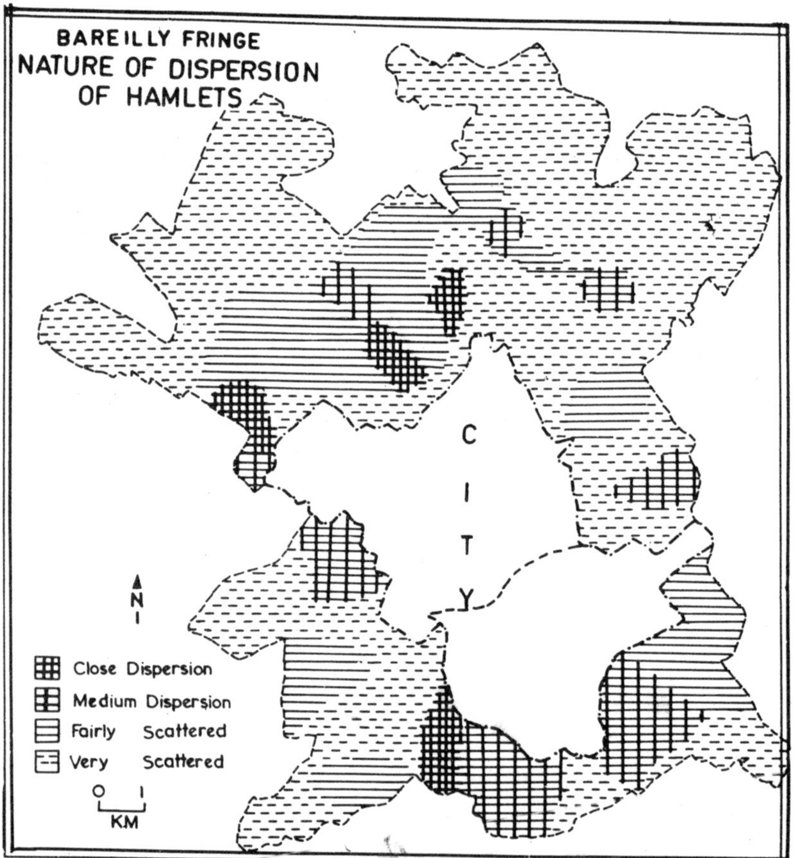

FIG. 5.5

PATTERN OF DISPERSION

On the basis of the number of hamlets, villages may be classified into three types, i.e., compact, semicompact and hamleted. It is found that nearly 82 percent of the villages are compact having equal number of hamlets. The semi-compact settlements, consisting of only 12 percent villages, have more hamlets than the number of villages but less than double the number of villages. Only 6 percent villages come under hamleted type having more than double the number of hamlet. These villages have more than 3 hamlets each. Thus, the main factors responsible for the high concentration of population and hence the growth of compact and semi compact settlements are connected with the exurbanite trend and nearless to the city centre. In some areas scattered houses are seen owing to abundant open land and constant building activity.

It is obvious from the above discussion that the area occupied by the hamlets and inter-hamlet distance increase with the increase of distance from the city centre (Tables.4). The area occupied by a hamlet doubles within the difference of only 4.5 Km. On an average, a hamlet occupies 104 hectare in sector two which increases to 220 hectare in sector four. It is noteworthy that the gradient of inter-hamlet distance, as it is clear from the graph, is less steep than the gradient of area occupied by a hamlet (Fig.5.2B). The nature of settlement dispersion is 'fairly scattered' in sector two and 'highly scattered' in other sectors. Thus it may be concluded that the people living in the peripheral villages (7.5 km to 9 km. from the centre) are living in widely spaced fairly compact clusters and at 4.5 to 6km. from the centre inhabitants are distributed among small but closely spaced hamlets.

TABLE 5.4 **Variation in settlement Dispersion by Distance Increase.**

Roads	Inter-Hamlet Distance in Metres (Kms. from city centre)				Average for the Ribbons
	3-4.5	4.5-6	6-7.5	7.5-9	
Bareilly-Rampur	1720	931	1191	1577	1406
Bareilly-Nainital	-	2009	896	1348	1418
Bareilly-Budaun	1541	1316	1761	1550	1542

The average figures of settlement dispersion by distance increase for all three ribbons (along the main routes) do not show any significant pattern of regression (Table.4).

This may be attributed to the fact that the importance of physical factors as determinanats of settlement pattern might have been greatly modified by the sociocultural and economic dominance of the urban centre of Bareilly.

GENERAL CHARACTERISTICS OF SETTLEMENTS

Most of the settlements of the fringe are predominantly rural in character. Their layout is wholly unplanned and the settlements are actually divided on the basis of caste and social groups. Some of the villages along the roads show different hemlets within the traditional revenue village boundary or'mauja' inhabited by different social-economic groups. The age-old cohesion in these villages seem to have under-gone such change more than those of the villages away from the city. This shows that the urban influence has penetrated into their ways of life and interrelationships, even if physical changes are slow to take place.

Economic factors, especially industrial location have played important role in giving rise to the growth and status of urban and market centres while ribbon developments along the highways are the direct result of city's interaction with the region through the highway. Even some of the compact villages,like Mohanpur and Kargauna have generated some satelite settlements along the highways (Fig. 5.6). There is a general tendency to convert the frontage of houses along the roads into some shopping, repair shops, tea stalls, etc. or other non-traditional uses. Thus, the land values along the road show a tremendous rise in anticipation of landuse conversion in future. Such trends are visibly expressed through the earmarked plots along such roads on the outer flanks of the rural settlement.

In other rural settlements which are not directly linked with roads, the impact of the town is visualized through changes in agricultural landuse. For example, in Theria Nizabat Khan, a typical village of this type, agriculture is oriented to market gardening, dairy and poultry farming mainly due to the avalibility of ready market in the town. Further, socio-cultural behaviour of the people of these villages are also changed. Mention may be made of education, dress and food habits in which positive changes are noticiable.

LOCATIONAL PATTERNS : SAMPLE VILLAGES

All the five sample villages are situated between a distance of 5 km. to 10 kms. from the city. Mohanpur and Kargaina are situated at a distance of 5 km. each, Khalilpur and Govindpur 6 km. each and Jauharpur 10 km. from Kutubkhana. These villages are situated on a levelled land. Except Govindpur, all these sample villages are situated on the main roads.

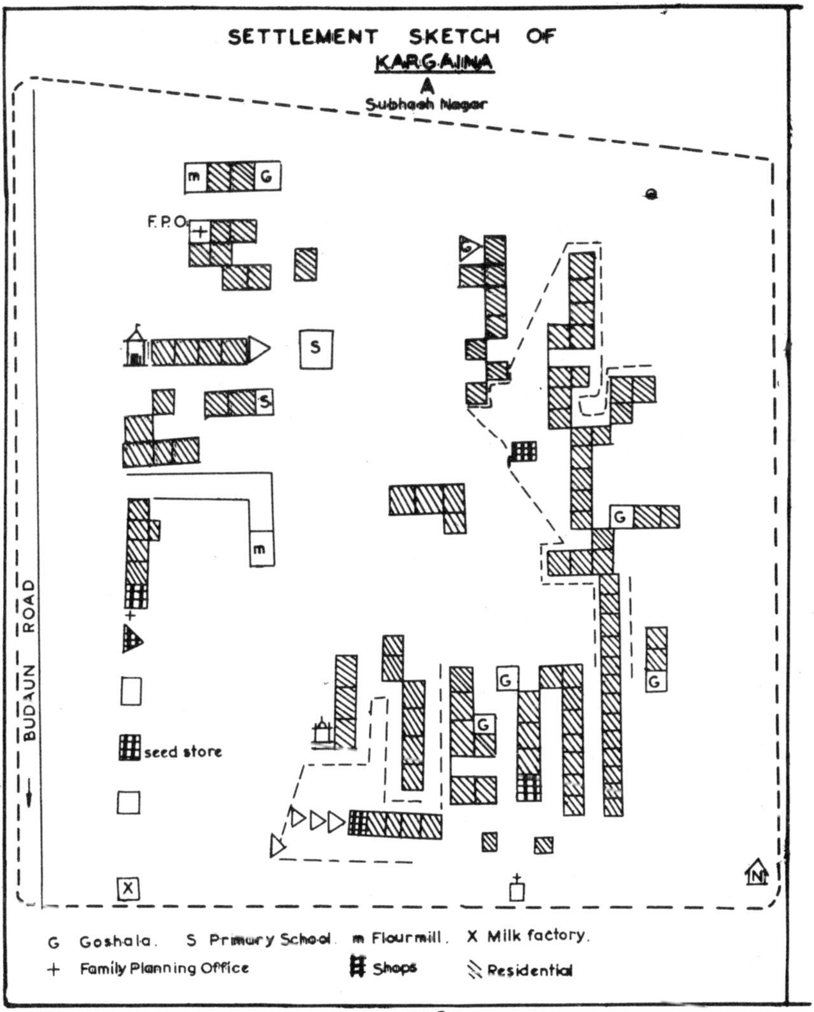

FIG. 5.6

Govindpur village is situated about 2 km. to the west of Nainital road. Khalilpur, having most of the manufacturing units of C.B.°Ganj area within its limit, spreads on both sides of the Bareilly-Moradabad road. It has most of its shops on one side of the road with industies and dwelling coming up in the northern side only recently. Same type of development is visible in Mohanpur along Bareilly-Shahjahanpur road. Except Mohanpur, all these villages are situated about two to four kilometers from the nearby railway stations. Khalilpur has direct city bus service while Govindpur, Jauharpur and Mohanpur are onbus routes, but the bus service is available at a distance of one and half Kilome ter away from the main village settlement.

Landuse record indicates that among these villages Kahlilpur (47.6 percent) and Jauharpur (38.2 percent) have higher percentage of their land under settlements while Kargaina and Govindapur have less than 10 percent of the area under settlements. The area under settlement increased from 7.8 percent to 10.1percent in Kargaina and 34.2 percent to 38.1percent in Jauharpur in between 1970-1980. Rest three villages show a nominal change of only one percent in the said period. The land under residential uses in Jauharpur and Kargaina has increased after the acquistion of land for non-agricultural uses e.g. in Kahlilpur and Nekpur respectively. Most of the development in these villages are taking place along the roads running through the village area.

Houses in the sample villages are generally madeup of mud and bricks combined. The old houses are made-up of mud while new construction is being made with brick and concrete. The change from the old to the new is explicitely evident in Mohanpur where settlement sites have just extended along Shahjahanpur road and majority of the houses are purcca. In Khalilpur and Jauharpur also the same feature is visible. However, a few of the houses are entirely pucca while others especially belonging to poor class, are kacha.

FUNCTIONAL CHARACTERISTICS

Kahlilpur and **Jauharpur** (Fig.5.7 & 5.8) lying on (Rampur road) about 6km. from Bareilly are being rapidly occupied by Clutterbuckganj industrial area. It has three large scale industries i.e., WIMCO, Rosin and Turpentine Distillery and Railway Sleeper Coach Factroy. Besides these, a camphor production unit, R.R. Group of industries, Polytechnic, I.T.I., an Industrial Estate alongwith residential quarters for officers and labourers, a model coloney for clerks and artisons, a hospital, Post and Telegraph Office, and Police outpost are some other important establishments. On account of these new establishments a ribbon type development has taken place along the road quite detached from the old rural settlement as well as the main industrial core. Vast barron and agricultural level land of Kahlilpur and Jauharpur has provided ample scope for future industrial development. Several brickkilns, small and medium sized manufacturing units such as R.S. Steelworks, Katha, Chemical, Camphor, bakelite, pencil production units in the industrial estate have come-up in the Jauharpur village. A coldstorage, three petrol pumps have also been installed here

Mohanpur along Shahjahanpur road and **Kargainaon** Budaun road are fast developing into a urban settlement on account of their being close to the city limit. Establishment of P.A.C. Camp has intiated a ribbon development in Mohanpur along the road. About 100 houses, mostly pucca, have sprung up here. They constitute a cold storage, a nature cure centre, P.W.D. store, a saw mill alongwith 20 shopsrelated to sweets, tea, tailoring haircutting washing as well as some private despensaries (Fig.5.9) and a number of brick Kilns. Post Offfice, a primary school and Junior high schools for boys and girls each are situated in the old premises of the village. There are a few private medical practitioners also in this village. About 25 percent houses are pucca and made of brick, cement and wood. It is an electrified village where 35 percent houses are having electric connections. Large number of government and Cantonment employees, artisans, businessmen and contractors reside in these settlements. Further growth of this type of settlement along this road is visualised by several dotted blocks of land earmarked as sites of different buildings.

Among the typical compact rural settlements of the fringe is **Kargaina** village lying in the south on Budaun association with the town. Most of the houses of thisvillage are pacca. There is a co-operative Milk Factory located in the south of the settlement area. Milk is collected from Anwala, Chandpur and Binawal villages. With 39 full-time workers, this factory produces skimmed milk, ghee, butter and cream which is being sold in the city. The village has a small market along the road where 8 grocery shops, 6 milk selling centres, 2 flour mills , 2 cycle reparing shops, blacksmith, hair cutting saloon, a co-operative seed store, 3 private medical practitioners and a family planning centre are catering the needs of the villagers and the surrounding area. A periodic market thrice in a week, is the speciality of this village (Fig. 5.6) Three grocery shops are scattered inside the old settement area. It has two primary schools to provide education to btoth boys abd girls sparately and a middle school for girls only.

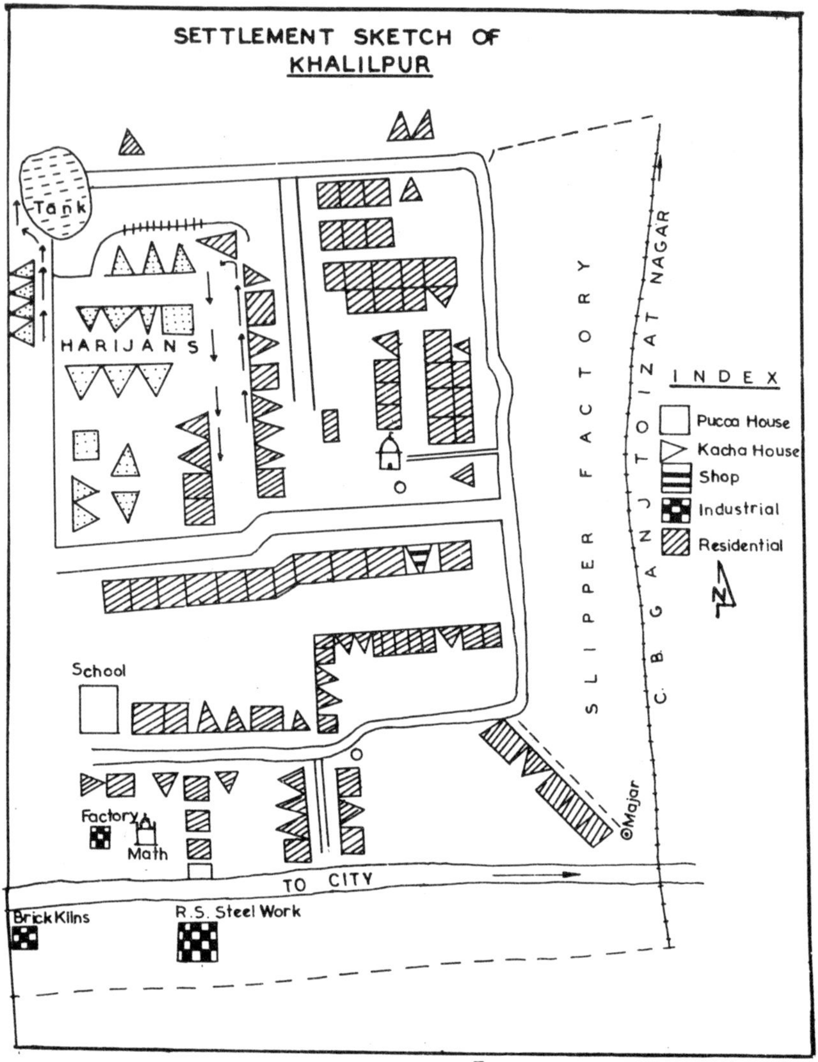

FIG. 5.7

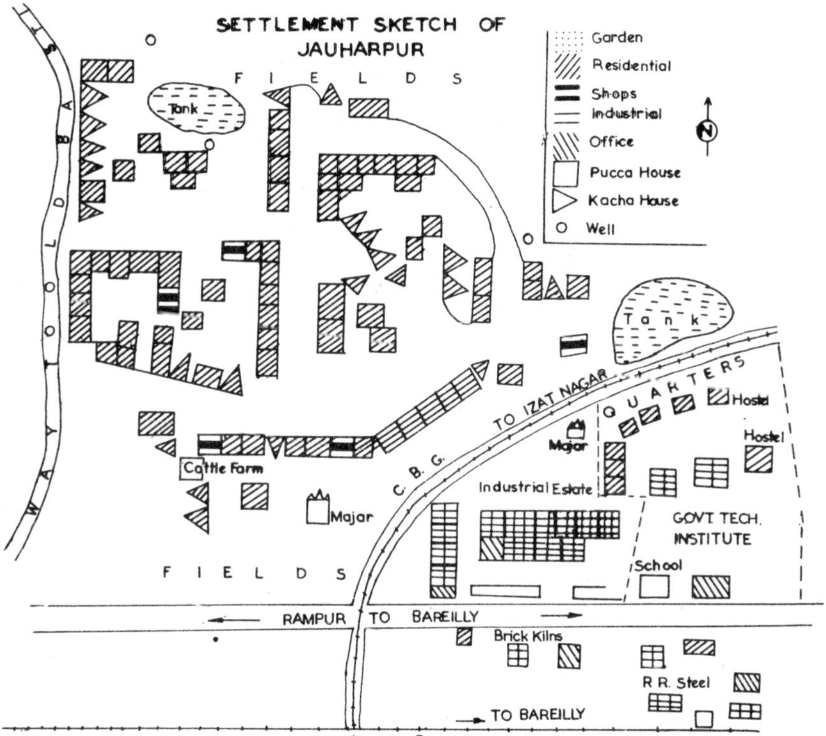

FIG. 5.8

The residents of the village are engaged either in cultivation of food grains or as in milk cattle rearing (with 5 cattleyards) as their secondary business. A few persons are employed in R.R.Co.,Faimily Planning Dept. and landrecord office. In the village boundary there are two brick-kilns mostly occupying agricultural land along west side of the road.

Govindpur lies at a distance of 3 km. to nearest motorable road and is situated west of the river Deorania. Due to its location in between Izatnagar and C.B. Ganjindustrial area, the settlement site of the village is fully compact. Most of the houses are kacha and give the impression of a dialapated and nested settlement. Basically the resident of this village are agricultural labourers and cultivators, about 25% of the labour force is engaged in construction work. Most of the houses are mainly residential. The living rooms are often turned into grain stores in the peack season. Nearly three of the buildings which have shops in the front room of their houses serve as residential cum-commerical structures. Besidesa, two of the buildings serve as primary school and one as community centre for the village. Some of the streets are paved with bricks. Most of them are quite narrow and hardly 2 to 3 meter wide.

In correlation with increasing distance from the city, outward appearance, structures and functions of settlements change from urban to rural in succession. Villages like Kareli, Govindpur and Bilwa appear more traditional while an impact of development and modernization is more evidents in settlements, such as Khalilpur, Jauharpur, Mohanpur and Kargaina etc.

LANDUSE PATTERN IN THE FRINGE

Expansion of urban built-up area upto the fringe and the changing use of land are among the most dynamic spatial processes of urban growth. Concersion of agricultural land to urban uses is a continous phenomena whose rate is stimulated due to the centrifugal forces of the city and its influence on the region. The land which is more amenable for conversion is that located adjacent to the city boundary, along arterial roads, near the already developed nodes in the fringe. The landuse pattern in the part of city's fringe is the result of several interreleated forces emerging from spatial and socio-economic structures and private and public decisions. The factors like accessibility, nature of the relief, distance from the city centre, increased transport facility, inefficinet control and lack of coordination among the developmental bodies have stimulated the conversion of agricultural land int urban uses.

The impact of Bareilly city on the fringe is highly reflected through the dynamic of landuses. Generally it is found that greater the physical contact of a settlement with the city, the more diversified are its landuses. Alongwith distance decay function operating on these dynamics, a number of factors outweigh the distance and accessibility factors in determining the landuses. In addition cultural elements such as caste structure, standard of education and the way of living together with physical elements like soil fertility, water supply and general character of land, play important rle in developing the type and intensity of landuse.

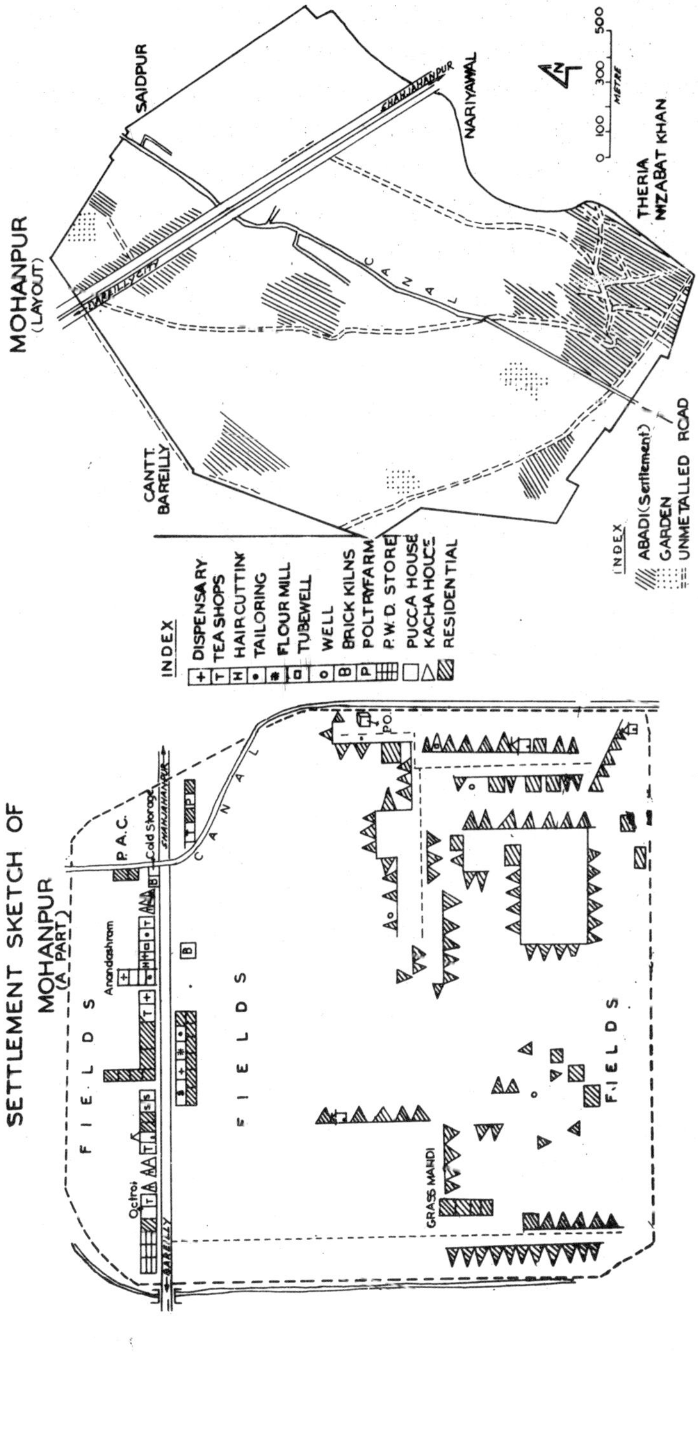

SETTLEMENT SKETCH OF MOHANPUR (A PART)
FIELDS
P.A.C.
Cold Storage
Anandashram
Octroi
BAREILLY
SHAHJAHANPUR
CANAL
GRASS MANDI
PO.
INDEX
DISPENSARY
TEA SHOPS
HAIRCUTTING
TAILORING
FLOUR MILL
TUBEWELL
WELL
BRICK KILNS
POLTRYFARM
P.W.D. STORE
PUCCA HOUSE
KACHA HOUCE
RESIDENTIAL
MOHANPUR (LAYOUT)
SAIDPUR
NARIYAWAL
THERIA NIZABAT KHAN
CANTT. BAREILLY
BAREILLY CITY
0 100 300 500
METRE
INDEX
ABADI (Settlement)
GARDEN
UNMETALLED RCAD

FIG. 5.9

The existing landuse pattern of Bareilly reveals a mixed type of land predominantly industrial in the north and north-west of the fringe (Fig.5.10). A comparatively lesser intensity of mixed land use is visible in the southern quarter of the fringe. The general landuse pattern is dominated by various agricultural and rural activities, as it forms more than two thirds of the total area of the fringe. Total land under agriculture and garden is about 83% of the total area while non-agricultural uses of the land is less than 17 percent.

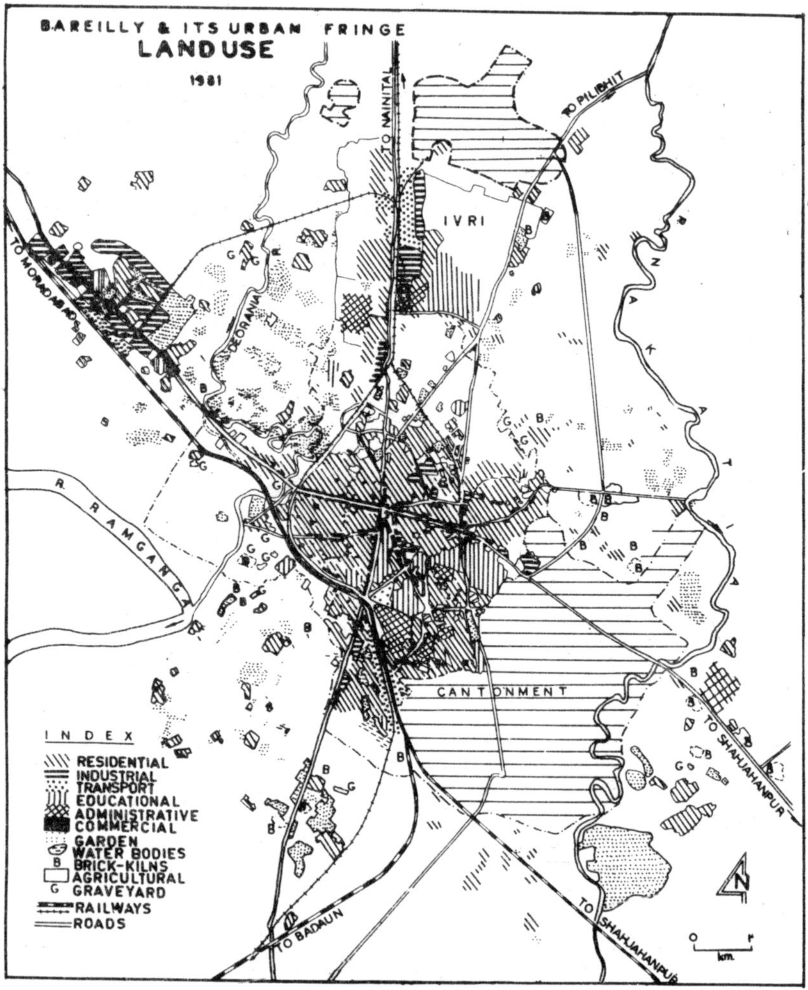

FIG. 5.10

In a strict sense, 59.5 percent of the land is under cultivation, 14.5 percent under settlements, 10.5 percent cultivable land, 9.7percent not cultivated, 3.6 percent under orchards and gardens and 2.2 percent as waterbodies. Being nearer to the city the villages take advantage of the city market by adjusting their land for growing vegetables, flowers and other cash-crops, though 80percent of the total agricultural land are on an average, still devoted to grains farming.

CHANGES IN LAND-USE PATTERN

Remarkable changes in landuse pattern are seen in this fringe between five year periood(Table 5.5).

TABLE 5.5 **Major land use of Urban Fringe (1975-1980)**

Uses	1974-75		1979-80	
	Area in Hect.	in %	Area in Hect.	in %
Builtup Area (Settlement etc)	1735	12.9	1923	14.5
Water bodies	430	3.2	282	2.2
Orchards/garden	363	2.7	484	3.6
Cultivated	7303	54.4	8002	59.5
Cultivable	1130	8.4	1412	10.5
Non-cultivated	2488	18.5	1304	9.7

Source : Based on Official village land Records, Tahsil, Bareilly.

The built-up area (including residential areas, roads, industries etc.) increased from 12.9 percent in 1974-75 to 14.3 percent in 1979-80. Several areas along the main roads radiating from the city were taken over by these non-agricultural uses during these years. The expansion of village settlement sites and the increases in the number of industrial units have been the sole factors in extension of the built-up area in the fringe.

The area under waterbodies on the other hand has fallen during these years due to the conversion of shallow water-logging areas into settlements and for brick-kilns sites etc. Area under all agricultural uses though has shown a 2 percent decrease in this period, the cultivated land has increased by 5 percent. Due to increasing pressure on land a decline in non-cultivated land from 18.5 percent to 9.7 percent is noticed during this period and this is responsible for the increase in garden (from 207 to 3.6%), cultivated land (from 54.3 to 39.5%) and cultivable land (8.4 to 10.5%). It has directly affected the cropping intensity of fringe villages (Fig. 5.11).

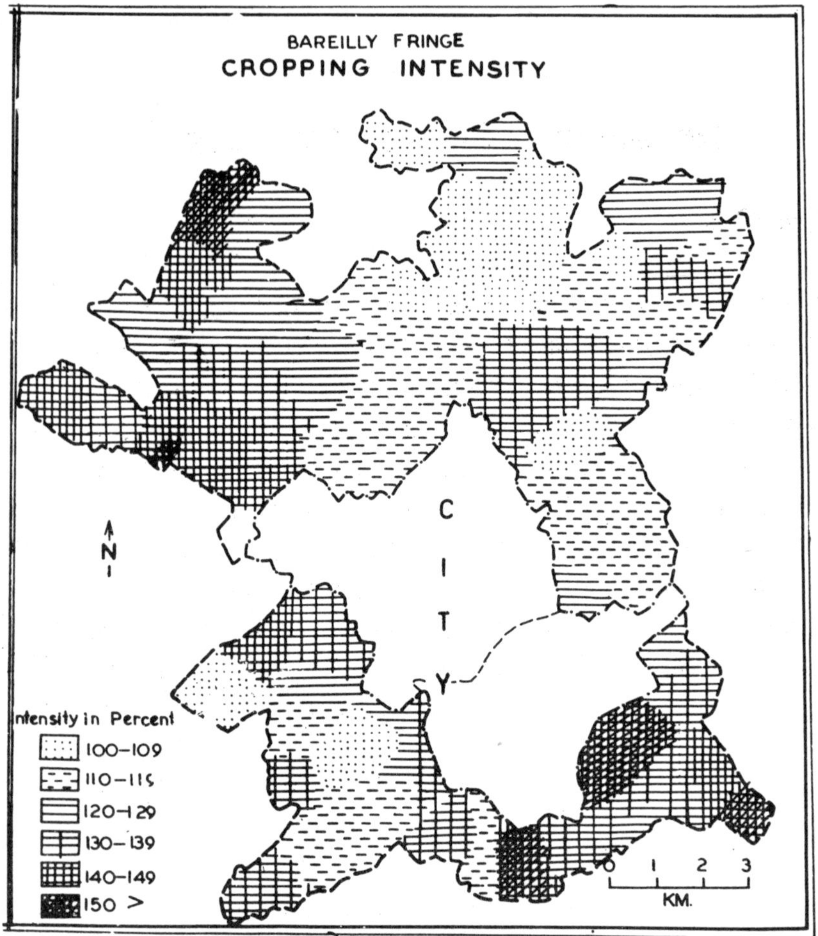

FIG. 5.11

The physical expansion of the city and its fringe is so diversified that the zones of landuse have varying intensity. Changes in landuse pattern vary at shorter distances in the south and east while the same level of variation takes place at larger distances in the west and northern fringe. The south-western lands, often inundated during rains, have a different character altogether.

Considering the pattern of landuse in the whole area in general and the sample villages in particular the impact of the urban centre of Bareilly is quite obvious. On the basis of sample villages some general characteristics have been visualized but the impact of the city is not the same everywhere, nor does it decrease in direct proportion with distance. The impact varies between the primary fringe and the secondary fringe. The primary or inner fringe is Characterized by changes in landuse, particularly expansion of settlements at the cost of other uses, most likely agriculture for urban expansion. The secondary or outer fringe is characterised by extensive landuses. In this zones single cropped land of the past is now converted int double and multiple cropping zoone.

Moreover, the degree oof landuse changes is not the same in all parts of the fringe. The north-west sector of the fringe has multiple uses mainly due to the fact that C.B. Ganj and Izatnagar outgrowths have influenced it cnsiderably. This area has better transprt facilities and provides better landfor future expansion (Fig.5.12). In the north of Bareilly-Moradabad Railway line, where new industries are coming up, buildings are being cnstructed along the road side right up to village Mathurapur, moostly at the cost of orchard and agricultural lands.

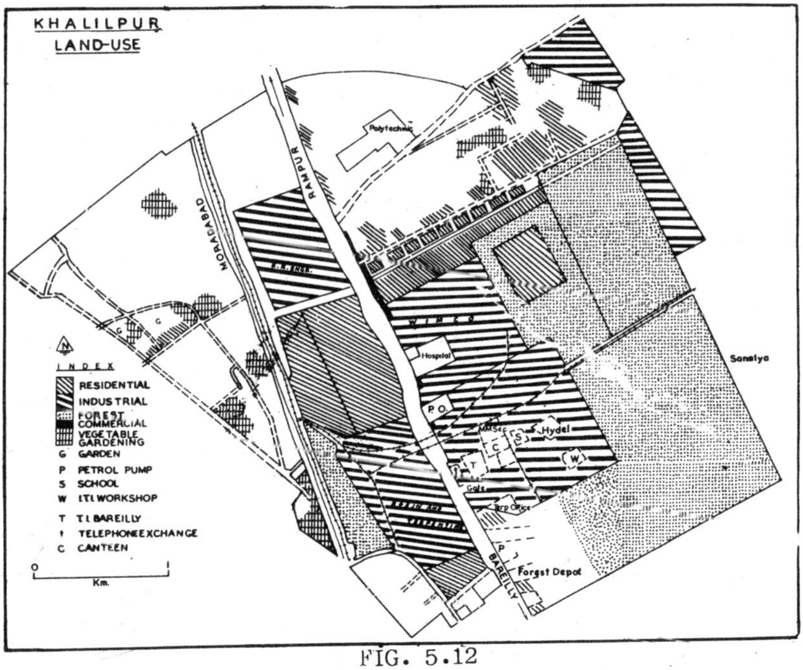

FIG. 5.12

The south-western fringe of the city present a different character. This area of the fringe, particulalry toward the Ramganga river, faces the problem of inundation, therefore the builtup area could not extend as much in this sectr as in north west sector. The intensity of landuse has increased along roadside oonly.

In the eastern fringe, which is very limited in area high mixed landuse intensity is visible only among one or two villages, especially along roadside. Further, innorth-east the existance of I.A.F. camp on a wider area with its restricted land has also influenced the land use pattern of the villages. Negligible changes have taken place in the eastern parts of the fringe extending upto the river Nakatia. Due to the lacl of transport facilities, this area is least accessible.

To conclude, the landuse pattern in the fringe focucces the changes in relation to industrial and residential developments. Whereas north, north-western sector shows multiple landuses, the south-west fringe has developed an extensive landuse on roadside. In the east while the southern part of the fringe has developed intensive agriculture, the northern part has more vacant land due to its location farther from the city centre.

SELECTED REFERENCES

1. Lal, H. (1972) Gradients of Urban Influence on the Rural SettlementConcentratin with special Reference to Bareilly, in R.L. Singh (Ed.) **Rural Settlements in Monsoon Asia.** NGSI pp 264-272.
2. Singh, V.R.. et.al. (1983) **Dynamish and Development in Rural and urban fringe...,**"Proceeding of the International Conference on Rural Develpment, Leige.
3. Sinha, MMP (1980) **The impact of urbanization on Land use in the Rural Urban Fringe**, Concept. New Delhi.

SIX

Public Utility Services

Public utility services and amenities have been added to the landscape of the city from time to time to serve the city and the fringe areas. These amenities are not in proportion to the phenomenal growth of population and the expansion of the city. Here in this chapter an attempt has been made to visualize the importance and impact of these services over the city's life.

Water Supply:

Earlier in both old and new cities the main source of drinking water had been brick-wells as the region has a high water table, i.e., only 6 metre (20 Feet) below the surface. Later on, hand pumps became popular as a means of water supply. Even today after the installation of municipal water supply works, handpumps are playing an important role in augmenting the supply of drinking water in most of the house of the city.

The administration of Bareilly Water Supply Scheme prepared and executed by the state L.S.G.E.D. at an estimated cost of Rs.24,00,000, was handed over to the Municipal Board in Jan, 1957. The water supply was commenced from April 1, 1957.

There has been a gradual development of Bareilly water works during the year 1958-59. About 1.75 km new water mains were laid in the town and 16 new standposts were erected during this period. The total number of water connections existing on 31.3.59 was 711.

Bareilly water supply scheme was first designed for an estimated population of 19,7000 at the rate of 25 gallons per head per day. It was reorganized for a projected population of 4,75,000 for years 1995 at the rate of 40 gallons per head per day to cope with the additional demands of the town due to the abnormal increase in population. According to the original supply scheme the town was divided into 5 zones, each zone has its own zonal overhead tank of 75,000 gallon capacity and two tubewells. The number of zones are proposed to be increased to 6 in Phase I and 8 in II and III phases each of 10 year's duration.

The total length of the pipe lines in the city in 1963-64 was 75 km. and approximate per capita per day water supply was 6.32 gallons. By the end of this decade average supply touched 20 lakh gallons.

Now the total area covered by water works system is 41 sq. kms. There are 37 fire hydrants and about 200 public stand posts, 3 cattle druffs and 14 connections for the municipal gardens. Total connections with metres is crossing 4000 (Bareilly M B Annual Administrative Report 1975-76).

DISTRIBUTION OF WATER SUPPLY BY WARDS

According to the socio-economic survey of the city, it has been found that only 25 percent of the households are having municipal taps. 3 percent households use public taps. Rest 70 percent households still use handpumps. It is mainly due to the fact that besides a big number of private handpumps municipal board also maintains 336 hand pumps in the city area.

Wardwise figures reveal that ward No.8 is best served with water supply and the mohallas of Chahbai, Bajaria Puran mal, and Gali Nawaban, have water connections in every dwellings. Ward Nos 1,3,4,6,7 and 5 (mostly in the inner zone) are having a considerable number of taps within their limits. Most of the outer areas of the city or the suburban zone have no water connections. Thus, Bareilly city has inadequate supply of water.

The Cantonment Board purchases water from the Military Engineering Services Waterworks and supplies it to the civilians also. The Board also maintains 37 public handpumps, 22 stand pipes and a hydrant on one of the roads for watercarts etc.

WATER SUPPLY IN THE URBAN FRINGE

Wells and handpumps are the main source of drinking

water in the fringe also. However 20 villages constituting of primary inner fringe are being served by tube wells. Most of the villages situated at the outer limit of the western fringe have only wells as a source of drinking water. In certain areas tank, river and canal water is used for drinking purposes.

All the big factories and mills situated beyond the municipal limits in Clutterbuckganj and Izatnagar area have their own piped water supply systems with tubewells and overhead tanks. So is the case of residential colonies and labour colonies developed in these parts (S E Survey, Bareilly, 1971). Thus in general, people in the fringe area still depend on primitive means of water supply.

DRAINAGE AND SEWAGE DISPOSAL

Bareilly city has no planned drainage or sewage system. A skeleton system of drains exist which leaves the sullage to stagnate abruptly forming pools in low lying area, without any outlet. During rainy season the sullage mixed with rain water flows along some of the main roads of Beharipur and Gulabnagar. Due to insufficient capacity of storm water-cum-sullage drains an extremely insanitary sight is presented.

Beharipur and Gulabnagar roads are along the natural water-shed forming a valley of nearly 1.5 km. in length. Here often such sights may be seen during rains.

RUBBISH AND NIGHT SOIL REMOVAL

Though the disposal of rubbish and night soil is in the process of being mechanized, most of the work is done by hand. The night soil is collected in the 'dalaos' which in the majority of cases are kacha without screen walls. Further, it is removed both by departmental agency and by contractors.

As city lacks sewer lines, the service types of latrines are common in whole of the town and a considerable part of new town. The night soil is removed by sweepers in baskets and Hand carts, who carry it to the dumping grounds. But recently with the development of partial sewage system and construction of sullage pits, this inhuman and unhygienic work is being abandoned. Lately the municipal board is using mechanical transport for removing night soil.

LAVATORY FACILITIES

In 1974 there were 4254 private latrines in which 4214 were of service type and 17 flush type. People in Mohallas Hussainbagh and Lodhitola are still using the open fields for easing themselves.

PROPOSED SEWERAGE SCHEME

The comprehensive drainage scheme is proposed to be executed in number of phases for a projected population of 475000 in year 1994. On the basis of topography the depth of sewer will be restricted to 6 metres deep only. The whole area of the town is divided into four zones: , main city, old city, north extension and Subashnagar. Each zone will have a pumping station in which sewerage will gravitate through a network of sewer's service area. Subashnagar pumping station will pump sullage to the common sewage farm where raw sewage will be utilized.

This project commenced in 1971 and in first phase pucca surface drains and nalah were erected in more than three fourths of the city. Arrangement was made to discharge the sullage smoothly in the Nakatia, Deorania and Ramganga rivers. A sullage farm was established in the South-West fringe of the town along Budaun road in 1976. This project is running successfully and is expected to be completed during 1985-86.

ELECTRIC LIGHT AND POWER SUPPLY

Before 1929, when the town was first served with electricity, Kerosene oil lamps were the main source of street illumination and even upto the end of the sixtees there were certain localities where lighting was done by means of such lamps. In 1964 there were 4376 electric street lamps and 2,000 kerosene oil lamps on the roads and streets of the city.

The Bareilly Electric supply Co. Ltd. commenced in 1928. In 1948, the city was connected with Sharda-Hydro-Scheme.

The electric distribution network to the city and Cantonment consists of about 120 Km. of low tension supply line fed through 20 transformers and three converting substations. The average connected industrial load of the city is 6204. 185 KW. distributed among 791 units.

Socio- economic survey of the city reveals that in 1971 there were only 38 percent of the houses electrified. Out of 13705 electric connections in Bareilly Urban Agglomeration, 1260 were industrial and 4379 commercial. Total road lighting points were 6218.

Out of 77 villages in the **fringe** 42 or 54 percent are electrified.

HEALTH SERVICES

Bareilly provides the general and specialized medical facilities for a fairly wide region. There are three general hospitals, namely Clara Swain, District and Dufferin Hospitals, having a total number of 565 beds. In all there are 19 hospitals and dispensaries of all kinds (Allopathic, Homeopathic, Ayurvedic and Unani) situated in the city. There are specialized hospitals and dispensaries treating in particular diseases. In addition to these, there are a good number of private practitioners found in almost all parts of the city.

Clara Swain Hospital, started in 1874, has 260 beds (of which 133 are for women), 16 private rooms and a staff of 17 doctors, 5 dentists, 6 compounders, 100 nurses and 125 other employees. The hospital is equipped with 5 X-ray machines, a mobile miniature X-ray van, a pathological laboratory and has facilities for diathermy. It treats about 5,000 indoor and 30,000 outdoor patients annually on average.

Dufferin Hospital established in 1889 but the government took it over in 1946. It is a woman's hospital with 54 beds and has facilities for X-ray, diathermy and pathological tests.

District Hospital which is a general hospital for both the sexes and has several sections: medical, surgical, orthopaedic, ear, nose and throat, dental, tuberculosis, pathology, radiology and children's. There are 159 beds of which 38 are for female patients. It is manned by 18 medical officer's, 15 compounders and 59 nurses. Average number of patients treated per day is 1075. Family Planning cell provides facilities to about 100 persons in a month.

The Mental Hospital, a government institution, is an old regional hospital having a very wide catchment area with a total 408 beds. (296 beds for men and 112 for women). It treats on an average 400 patients in a year.

The Eye Hospital (1951) is a branch of the Sitapur Eye Hospital. Under the control of a chief medical officer, this has 170 beds and a staff consisting of two doctors, two compounders and 5 nurses.

Infectious Diseases Hospital, Bareilly, managed by municipal corporations has 6 beds under the charge of a medical officer, a compounder and two others.

Family Planning Centres: Under District Hospital, there are 14 family planning centres, working in different part of the district. Recently a mobile vasectomy team (with headquarters at Bareilly) has been added to provide facilities of sterilization among men and its area of operation included the Bareilly and Kumaun regions.

The maternity and child welfare activities of the city is functioning at Kutubkhana and Shahmatganj centres. Dufferin and Claraswain Hospitals have 20 and 18 beds providing maternity services to the city. The scheme of free distribution of skimmed milk to expectant and nursing mothers is running since 1954. On an average 540 mothers and an equal number of children are benefitted under this programme every year.

The Government health school for the training of health visitors has been functioning in the city since 1956. Apart from these there are 5 restricted hospitals: North Eastern Railway Hospital-Izatnagar, Police Lines Hospital-chaupala, Central Jail Hospital and Kishore Sadan Hospital (Juvenile Jail)-Izatnagar, which provide medical facilities for railway employees, police and prisoners respectively.

There are 6 charitable dispensaries which are scattered in different parts of the city. Among these 5 are reserved for their own employees. The Municipal Aurvedic Aushadhalaya is the only dispensary in public sector situated near Quila Subji Mandi.

The total number of beds in these hospitals are only 997 which is not adequate for the population of the city. The number of beds per 1000 of persons in 1971 come about 2.78 while the same figure for developed countries are more than 10. The hospitals are not evenly distributed in the city. Most of the hospitals are located in Civil Lines only.

PREVENTIVE MEASURES AND CONTROL OF DISEASES

In the city, some of the killing diseases like smallpox, cholera and plague have been totally controlled by different preventive measures, such as compulsory inoculation and vaccination etc. There are all 6 enoculators and vaccinators, but in relation to growing number of population their number appears to be inadequate. Maleria which was eradicated in past, again raising its head. It needs strong measures to eradicate the mosquito menance areas by constant spraying of DDT and other insecticides.

TRANSPORT AND COMMUNICATION

An efficient pattern of circulation is an important requirement of the urban communities for its proper functioning. Circulation network links different parts of the city together and keeps the entire urban community into one compact unit. The pattern of the network of the roads and streets has emerged with the trend of development of the town and is a function of its landuse.

Existing Road System : Bareilly has grown on the cross roads of G.T. Road and the Chaupala-Pilibhit Road. Both of these roads are the principal old roads of the town. The entire old town lies in the segments of these cross-roads. The Pilibhit Road beyond the Barabazar Crossing in the north bifurcates into old Pilibhit and Nainital Road and similarly the Barabazar road also bifurcates at its eastern end to Bisalpur Road and Shahjahanpur Road. Besides these roads numbers of other narrow lanes criss-cross the entire older built-up parts of the city meeting these roads (fig. 1.7).

Construction of N.E. Railway track along the western side of the city have further limited and governed the road pattern of the town. A road has been constructed along the entire length of the railway track and encircles the eastern half built-up part of the town.

The south-eastern segment of the town has, however developed in planned way to a certain extent and forms the civil lines area. The road meeting the Barabazar road through the Civil Lines and Cantonment with the central hub of the city. A number of roads connect this road with various work centres and the other major landuses in the Civil Lines. The national highway No. 24 running in east-west direction and meeting the hospital road at the Ayubkhana crossing forms another axis of development parallel to Barabazar road.

COMPOSITION OF TRAFFIC VOLUME

Traffic survey data reveals that the highest volume of traffic is on Novelty talkies crossing. The maximum incoming and outgoing traffic (8 hourly) is carried by the Kutubkhana road at this crossing with 26858 vehicles. Next comes the Kutubkhana crossing which is located in the centre of the city.

It is also observed that at all the crossings the percentage of cycles are highest as it is the main means of private transport.

At Company Bagh crossing the composition of traffic is dominated by fast moving heavy vehicles. The incoming fast moving vehicles on this road were 2648 whereas cycles and other slow moving vehicles were 2350 and 1091 respectively in the year 1974.

PEAK HOUR TRAFFIC

An analysis of the traffic figures at 15 minutes interval, it is seen that the traffic is at its peak between 10-11 in the morning and 5-6 in the evening in the case of the majority of the intersections.

The highest per hour traffic is marked at Novelty Talkies crossing. On the Kutubkhana road in the east the average per hour traffic is calculated 3357 while in the west on Civil Lines road it is only 2656. This crossing handles the maximum volume of traffic in Bareilly as the road passes through commercial zone of Kutubkhana and by the side of different government offices, railway junction, collectorate and the residential areas of the Civil Lines etc.

Kutubkhana crossing is the next busiest crossing. Due to prohibition on heavy vehicles, the percentage of fast moving vehicles is very low in this central business core. A greater number of cycles from this crossing move to Nainital road for marketing and to attend different offices at Izatnagar. The same amount of traffic composed of rikshaw and cycles takes the direction of Barabazar and Quila along which the major retail market of the city is situated.

Further, kalibari road is the next higher peak hour traffic generating road due to the existance of wholesale grain market, roadways bus station, municipal board and other commercial centre.

A comparative figure of following table 1 reveals that cycle is the most prominent mode of transport with 75 per cent and above. Rikshaw comes next with more than 20 per cent of the total vehicles.

TABLE 6.1 **Peak Hour composition of Traffic Volume on Novelty & Kutubkhana crossings.**

Types of Vehicles	EVENING No. of Vehicles %				MORNING No of Vehicles %			
	NC	KC	NC	KC	NC	KC	NC	KC
Truck & Bus	32	2	0.5	-	23	5	0.6	0.1
Car	137	67	2.2	1.6	130	47	3.2	1.1
Auto-cycle	241	103	3.8	2.5	173	116	4.2	2.6
Rikshaw	916	1363	14.5	33.0	1296	914	31.4	20.7
Cycles	4950	2535	78.4	61.3	2460	3273	59.6	74.2
Others	39	67	0.6	1.6	43	56	1.0	1.3
Total	6315	4137	100.0	100.0	4125	4401	100.0	100.0

Source : Volumetric and Direction Survey, Bareilly, 1971
NC = Novelty Talkies crossings, NC = Kutubkhana crossing

CITY-BUS SERVICES

Rapid urbanization with resultant increase in administrative, business and commercial activities have made it necessary for the large segment of population to depend upon mass transit system. The U.P. Govt. Roadways started its services in Bareilly city in 1950 by covering kutubkhana-Bareilly junction route. In 1960 there were 4 buses plying on the city roads and by 1964 another 6 buses were added. By 1963-64 the service had been extended on two more routes - Koharapir, Bhojeepur and to Fatehganj. On an average only 5,000 passangers travel daily by city bus and for greater number of passangers had to take the other means of transport.

Due to narrow width of roads **cycle-rikshaw** are the only convenient means of transport in the city at present. Among other vehicles cycle appears to be the most important means of transport (Table-2). As many as 61.7 per cent to total number of vehicles are cycles. Next comes cycle-rikshaw with 23 per cent of the total number of vehicles. Tonga which was important means of transport in early days are disappearing fast and total number in 1978-79 was 182 (only 1% of the total). Bullock cart, handcart and thela are generally used for goods transportation within the city, while the number of bullock-cart and handcart had declined a little within last few years, number of four wheeled **thelas** have improved slightly (6.4% of the total). It means the city still has to depend on old system of conveyance.

TABLE 6.2 **Yearly movement of the vehicles in the city**

	1974-75	%	1976-77	%	1978-79	%
Cycle	9265	61.3	11628	65.0	11800	61.7
Rikshaw	3489	23.0	3945	22.1	4692	24.6
Tonga	196	1.3	214	1.2	182	1.2
Bullock Cart	417	2.8	486	2.7	463	2.4
Handcart	653	4.3	628	3.5	726	3.9
Thela (4 Wheel)	1082	7.2	986	5.5	1237	6.4
Total	15102		17887		19110	

Source : Municipal Board, Bareilly.

ORIGIN AND DESTINATION OF TRAFFIC

Most of the traffic is routed towards major work centres of the city situated in Civil Lines, Barabazar and Shahmatganj market areas, C.B. Ganj industrial area and the Izatnagar railway township. Maximum number of trips are performed from the heavily congested wards of the city to the above mentioned work centres generally located on the outer fringe. The concentration of work centres at a fewer locations, therefore, necessiates longer journeys causing the acute traffic problems (Fig. 6.1).

GOODS TRAFFIC

The transport of goods in bulk has been undertaken by the railways since their introduction into the city in 1873. In the eighteenth and nineteenth centuries riverine transport was utilized as it was cheap and convenient for the transporting of heavy goods and materials. A great shortage of wagons for transporting goods other than war materials during the war of 1939-45 led to the introduction of motor trucks for this purpose and as this mode of transport was found to be most useful and convenient, it has continued in service. The facility of loading and unloading trucks and lorries at any point on the route and advantage of door to door service together with minimum breakage or loss have given it an edge over the railways. Bareilly being an important trading centre, 1700 public carriers and 150 private carriers were in service in 1980-81.

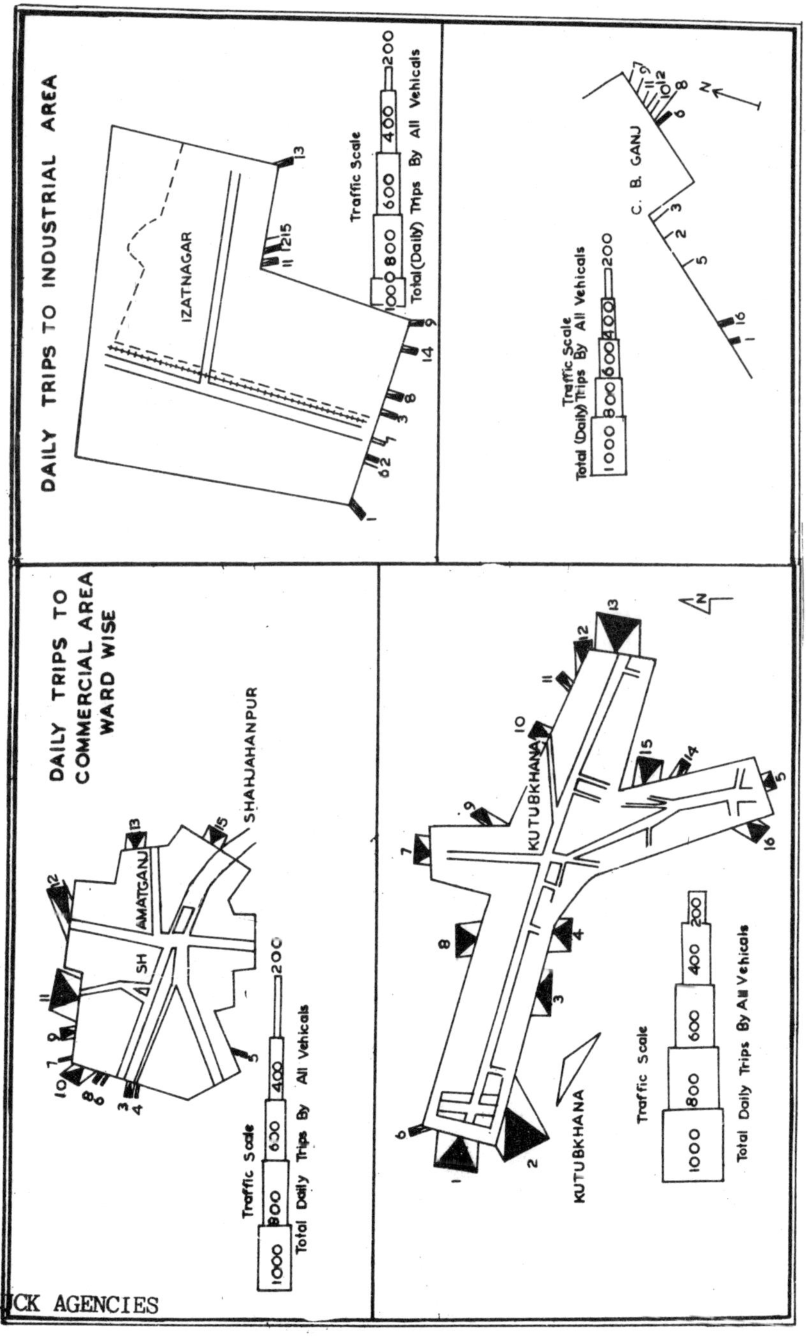

TRUCK AGENCIES

FIG. 6.1

Truck agencies in Bareilly are located on Shahjahanpur, Rampur, Pilibhit and Nainital roads. Concentration of agencies are mostly at Shahmatganj and Lichibag (Quilla) the well known grain markets of Bareilly. There are no proper and definite provisions of truck terminus in this city as such the trucks are parked on roadsides in congested commercial areas for loading and unloading of goods. Thus they create more congestion and bottlenecks.

RAILWAY GOODS TRAFFIC

The town is served by two railway systems, the broadgauge connects the city to Delhi in the west and Lucknow on the east. A narrow gauge railway line joines the city through Izatnagar to the northern part of foot hill of Himalaya and Kumaun region. Thus commercially it is very well placed taking the advantage of plain as well as the hilly track. It has affected the commercial activity of Bareilly which is the main centre of furniture industry.

Since 1961, the railways have been carrying large quantities of goods in and outside the city. A full-fledged yard is being developed at the Bhitaura railway station on the broadgauge. Similarly the transporting and storing capacities of the Clutterbuckganj and Chaneti railway stations are being expended. The transshipment of goods at Bareilly junction is done through six broadgauge and three metregauge lines. In addition to skilled manual transshipment an electric gantry crane has been installed.

MEANS OF COMMUNICATION

Postal services were opened about the middle of the 19th century, but till 1908 the system did not work properly. Since then a number of post offices were opened in the city and today the number has increased to 108. The G.P.O. is located in the centre of the town, near Kutubkhana.

Similarly, there are 8 telegraph offices located in the city in addition to the telegraph services of railway stations. The town is served by the telephones but greater part of the town is unserved by the telephone. Thus, the services of communication in Bareilly in modern context appears to be poor.

PARKS

The parks and gardens are considered to be lungs of the town and there should be enough space reserved for them. In all there are only seven parks in the city. The Gandhi Garden or the City Garden is the main park of the city which covers a vast area in the southern end of Civil Lines near Circuit House. It has a good nursery, two lawns, and a few flower beds. Jubilee Park or company garden is also an extensive park situated in the upper portion of the Civil Lines in front of M.Board Office. There is a social welfare centre, a club building a reading room and some play courts for special games. In addition, there are smaller parks and are maintained by the municipal corporation at different crossings.

The newly developed areas are planned and have enough open spaces and parks. Rampur garden area, Model town Shahdana, deserves special mention. Phoolbagh in cantonment is also a big park with several sections.

PLAYGROUNDS

A sport stadium is located on Pilibhit road in an isolated place. Bareilly college, Govt. Inter college and Islamia college have their own play grounds. Pared ground in civil lines, Police Line's play ground near District Jail, Ramlila ground near Gulab Rai Inter College in the north are used as local playgrounds.

As already discussed in chapter four the number and area under these amenities are in-adequate.

CULTURAL FACILITIES

LIBRARIES

The town does not possess any library that needs special reference. Govt. District library situated on Kutubkhana-Junction road is the only public library. There are three other libraries, welfare (Sufitola) Imdad library (Beharipur) and Ragia (Sailani) where a few hundred books and some leading newspapers and magazines are available. These libraries serve their own localities or communities.

In addition to these, all the colleges, P.G. and degrees, Inter colleges and few high schools as well as many professional colleges have their own libraries for their own students. Bareilly college Library, and IVRI Post Graduate

Institute library are the biggest in the region.

RECREATIONAL CENTRES AND CINEMA HOUSES

There is a great dearth of recreational facilities in Bareilly. The only park providing facilities for some sort of recreation to the youth is Jubilee Park. There is a few clubs in the civil lines whose members are generally government officers and few lawyers and business persons.

In all there are 11 cinema houses in the city. About half dozen picture palaces are concentrated on Motilal Nehru road around Novelty talkies crossings near Kotwali, the newly developed business area.

There are 14 dharmshalas scattered in the older part of the city, the important ones being the municipal sarai and the Khunni Lal which charge a nominal rate for accomodation. Some of the better known hotels and lodging houses in the city of Bareilly are the Bareilly, civil and military, Royal, Tirose, East Light and Ajanta; all of which are located within 4 Kms of the Bareilly railway station. The public works department maintains an inspection house, a circuit house and two dak bungalows. Other departments, like canal, opium, forest, Railways and soldier's, have their respective rest houses scattered in Bareilly city, C.B. Ganj and in Izatnagar.

City has not come up as a tourist centre in the map of U.P. Being a centrally located town near the northern hills, it may be an important tourist attraction provided better halting facilities are provided to the tourists.

SEVEN

Problems and Planning

Like the cities of the west, Indian cities have also experienced an unprecedented increase of population within last few decades. All the big cities of U.P., including Bareilly have seen a tremendous growth of population within the last three decades. This gain in population has presented several problems of haphazard and imbalanced development which call for a sound base for restructure, reconstruction and planning.

It is obvious from the foregoing analysis that Bareilly and its urban fringe exhibit far less satisfactory conditions of living, economy and resourcefulness than what are warranted in the present age of science, technology and planning. The appalling congestion in the inner zone of the city, acute shortage of houses, traffic congestion due to heavy traffic on the narrow and winding roads and lanes, unsatisfactory health and medical services, undesirable and misuse of urban lands and lack of civic amenities are some of the most unfortunate deficiencies of this diseased city. The patient has reached a stage when pills and drugs will be of little help. It needs careful diagnosis by a board of experts and planned surgical treatment through the hands of efficient planners.

MAIN PROBLEMS OF THE CITY

Unsatisfactory housing conditions with its resultant slums and social decay and misuse of land, traffic congestion and environmental pollutions are some of the most important problems of this city.

TRAFFIC CONGESTION

The problem of traffic and transport in Bareilly is

largely the result of the phenomenal growth of its population and concentration of economic activities in a much smaller area. The increased economic activities have placed an increasing demand of efficient and cheaper means of transportation. The average speed with which the traffic moves along the Kutubkhana and Barabazar Road, is often blocked due to heavy traffic. The root cause of traffic congestion in the city is the inherited road network of the past with narrow and frequent intersections, which has now become obsolete in design and capacity to satisfactorily cater the demands of the present volume of traffic and the type of vehicles.

In the absence of proper and adequate space for loading, roadsides are generally used for loading and unloading the goods. This has reduced the valuable space along the road pavements. Lack of such conveniences are highly felt in the Shahmatganj wholesale area and the Barabazar, the principal markets of the city.

The width of major traffic arteries are extremely narrow in comparison to the volume of traffic carried by them. This has created congestion resulting in excessive delays and wear and tear of the vehicles. The width of Barabazar itself is as narrow as 5 metres and no where it is more than 12 metres.

Encroachment on roads is another serious problem that hampers the safe and easy movement of traffic. It is but natural that when the shops are too small to carry out the business transactions they will encroach upon the footpaths. A number of shops carryout their business on footpaths. Such conditions are generally marked along the Hospital Road. Shops in the main markets have suffered maximum encroachments. In many cases footpaths are not provided along the roads. Therefore the encroachments make the lanes still narrower and create serious traffic congestion. In Shahmatganj and Kalibari, trucks and thellas use the roadside for parking and loading-unloading of grains too.

The location of the district hospital in the busiest part of the town near Kutubkhana is also a cause of traffic congestion in the morning and evening due to large numbers of visitors. The location of vegetable market (Subzi Mandi) in this area is also a factor of traffic bottleneck at peak hours of the day. The railway level crossings at different places usually gets the traffic blocked when shunting takes place.

HOUSING PROBLEMS

Shortage of housing accommodation is a chronic disease of the city. The ratio of about 8 persons per room represents most unsatisfactory situation. Like other ill-fated cities of the state, Bareilly has been the prey of both private and public neglect.

A comparison of population and house increase in the city for the last three decades indicates that housing accommodation (140%) has not kept pace with the increase in the population (154%). This has naturally resulted in overcrowding. On an area of 25.36 sq.km within Bareilly, M.B. there are 38710 (1971) residential houses which give a density of 15.2 buildings per hectare (in 1981 it is 13.0).

It has been estimated that the average number of persons residing in a house is 7.7 (1971) (in 1981 6.9). Maximum intensity is marked in the inner zone around commercial belt as low incomegroup people live there in order to reduce the burden of the house rent. On the other hand Cantonment, Civil Lines and Izatnagar are the areas of lowest house density (Fig. 7.1). As far as room accommodation is concerned, 38 per cent of the city's population live in one room, 30.6 per cent in 2 rooms and 14.5 per cent in 3 rooms.

Occupancy rate index shows that the wards 8 and 9 are the best in terms of living space with a high percentage of 3 rooms and above dwelling units. Baquarganj of ward No. 1 is most overcrowded.

The condition of buildings of the city also warrant proper analysis. It is an obvious measure of blight and slum conditions. It has been observed that except the ward No. 3, all other peripheral wards present most delapidated housing condition with 82 per cent to 100 per cent kacha structures.

THE SLUMS

A slum is understood to be an area of overcrowded, squalid, closely built and unhygienic housing. Basically an area of darkness, despair and poverty is generally regarded as slums. The lower class residential areas of the city are scattered throughout the city in the form of slums.

According to a survey conducted in 1971 by socio-Economic Survey of Bareilly, there were 44 slum localities

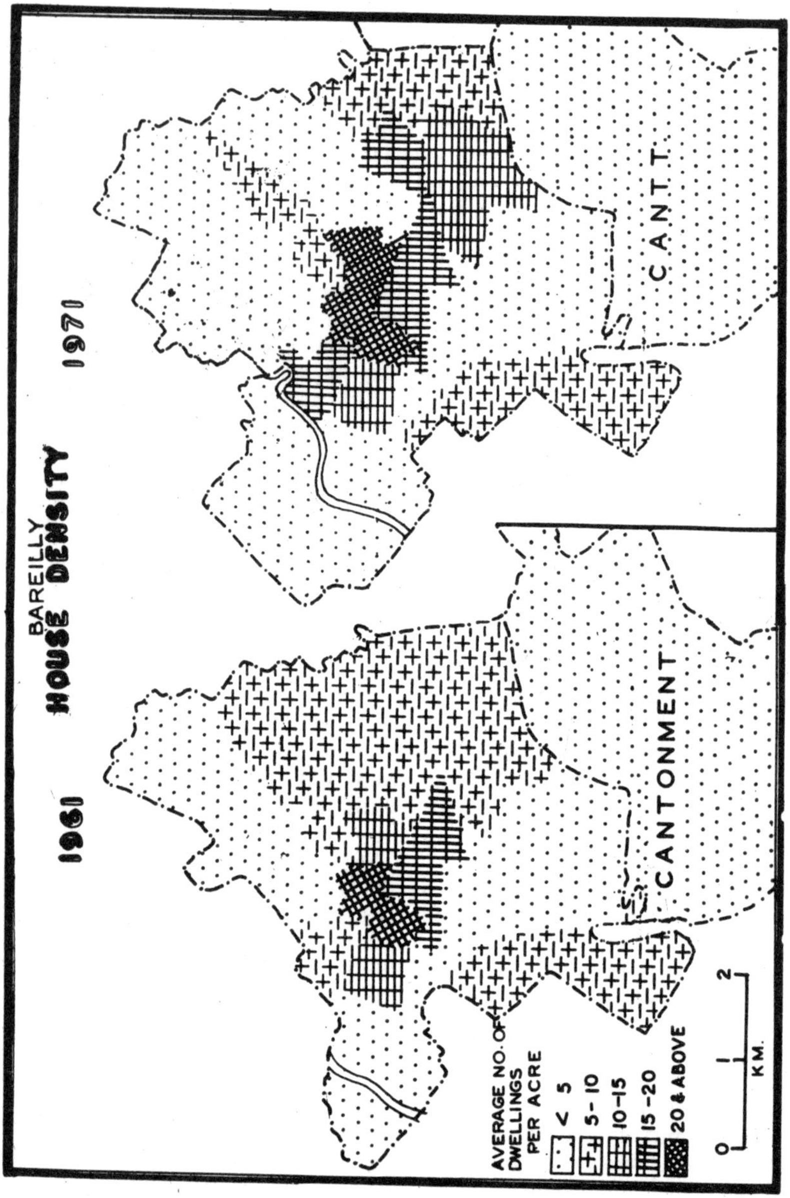
BAREILLY
HOUSE DENSITY
1961
1971
CANTONMENT
CANTT.
AVERAGE NO. OF DWELLINGS PER ACRE
< 5
5-10
10-15
15-20
20 & ABOVE
0
1
2
KM.

FIG. 7.1

in the municipal limit of the city. In all 96,000 persons constituting 29 per cent of the city's population lived in these slums. These slums are generally one room tenements, very often kacha. Regarding the occupancy status of slum dwellers, it was found that most of the slums dwellers have illegally occupied government or nazul lands. These slum localities had developed haphazardly, presenting an unpleasant look of the poor inhabitants living in squalid surroundings.

These dwellers are low paid and work as domestic servants, labourers, riksha and thela pullers, cycle repairers, bakers, washermen, barbers, shoerepairers, sweepers and brick-kiln labourers etc. It may be pointed out that the poverty dragged them to live in such conditions and also to push them into indebtness, illiteracy, anti-social activities and fatal diseases.

Due to absence of proper drainage, water logging is frequent. Narrow and dingy lanes and streets with insufficient lighting and ventilation appear more filthy by throwing of the rubbish and cowdung on the road itself. Inadequate number of public or private latrines compel residents to use nearby fields, more often even side and corner of roads, for easing themselves shamefully.

Two such localities are to be seen in Chandra Nagar on Rampur road and Nekpur on Budaun road. Both these squalid settlements are the result of their peripheral location near the industrial centres. In addition to these, some other villages formerly located on the outer fringe of the city and now completely engulfed by the city from all sides, have turned into big slum-pockets. The poor immigrants of rural areas found the cheapest accommodation of their taste in these villages whose population has multiplied 4 to 5 times within the last four decades. There are about 20 such pockets scattered mostly in the north-eastern and northern part of the city.

Lastly it is worth mentioning that there are some temporary hutments and shelters which have been erected by poor people, sometimes along the main roads even in the main part of the city. The majority of these hutments are of beggars and squatters, and when in group they form a regular bustee. One can found an example of such group of hutments on the Chaupala road leading to city Railway Station. In fact the condition of living in the inner zone of the city are far from satisfactory and the whole of the area may be designated as slums requiring immediate redevelopment and rehabilitation.

Urban Sprawl beyond the corporation limit is creating another problem. Relatively cheaper and tax-free land on the main fringe roads linked with the main city through mechanised transport have attracted several individuals and enterprenures for their investments primarily towards industrial sector. These uncontrolled developments where no building laws are in operation, are likely to create slums even at the outer rim of the city.

The industrial units established within congested residential localities, commercial areas etc. are functioning at the cost of the health and hygiene of the people. The development of sites in terms of coverage, accessibility, loading-unloading and parking facilities etc. is highly out dated and suffer from non-availability of space for expansion.

Similarly the government offices, an important work centres for the people of Bareilly have developed in an unplanned manner and are unevenly distributed in the residential areas. They are also responsible for further congestion of traffics, etc.

PROBLEMS PERTAINING TO PUBLIC UTILITY SERVICES

Overall improvement and development in the public utility services, such as, water supply and sewage facilities, are the pressing needs of the city. Improvement in the health and medical services, removal of educational and cultural backwardness are some of the leading problems of the city. The insanitary and unhygienic condition of different areas, the lack of open spaces, the scarcity of parks, playgrounds and public places pose several problems to the city dwellers.

The total land developed in the form of parks and playgrounds available per 1000 of people is about 0.20 hectare showing thereby an acute deficiency of open spaces and playgrounds for the people. No hierarchy has been maintained in the provision of parks and open spaces in Bareilly. As a result there are no children and other smaller sized parks provided at the neighbourhood level to meet the needs of the younger groups of population. Narrow streets, lanes and small squares are the only places where children often play. The insanitary conditions prevailed in these streets are highly hazarduous to their health.

ENVIRONMENTAL POLLUTION

The term refers to a wide range of forms of pollution of air, water and land. In this air pollution is the most significant form of environmental pollution. There are two principal sources in the city: motor vehicles and industrial processes. Pollution from motor vehicles pervades the whole city, though it is highly concentrated in the inner core because of the greatest concentration of vehicles there. Industrial air pollution is more localized and is virtually restricted to parts of the north-east and south western areas of the city.

THE AWAKENING TO THE PROBLEMS

It is a matter of some relief that the people and the authorities concerned have begun to realize the ills of the city and there is an awakening to the problem. The Improvement Trust established in 1963, in addition to general improvement, it reclaimed about 500 hectares of land for the construction of houses between Pilibhit and Nainital roads. The U.P. Government under its Regulation of Building Operations Act III, (1958) announced regulated area of Bareilly including 198 new villages around the city. The Town and Country Planning Department opened its survey division at Bareilly in 1968 to prepare a master plan for Bareilly.

THE PROPOSED MASTER PLAN FOR BAREILLY

The Master Plan for Bareilly was prepared on a long term basis for the next 25 years (1971-1996) keeping in view the future growth of population, economic development-potentials and technological-industrial advancements, likely to come during plan period. It aims to ameliorate the shortcomings of the past, to allocate areas for residential, industrial and commercial uses alongwith basic community facilities in right amount within the framework of socio-economic conditions of the future urban community. The ultimate objective is to make the plan functionally related, economically sound and socially desirable. This Master Plan (Fig. 7.2) was completed in 1971 and handed over to the municipal authority and there by to Bareilly Development Authority for its implementation. The following is the short summary of the Master Plan.

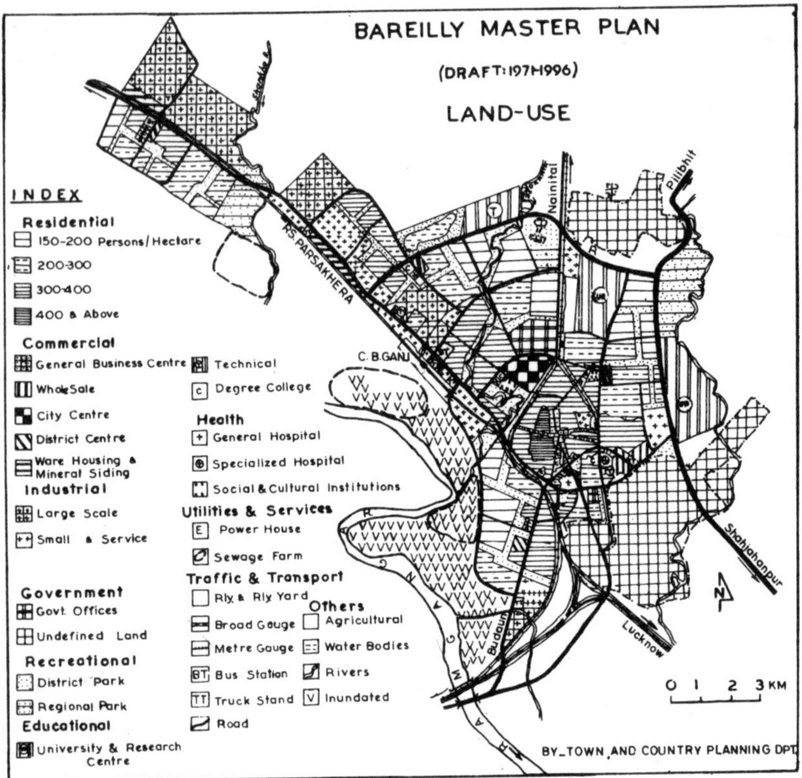

FIG. 7.2

CHARACTERISTICS FEATURES

The population of Bareilly is expected to grow to a size of about 9,25,000 by the end of next 25 years. The present area under municipal limit will not be able to meet the requirements of this increase in population, therefore new areas will have to be found to take up future urbanization of Bareilly. Considering different factors the regulated area was demarcated and it was found that there was enough scope for the growth of city to north, north-east and south-west part of the city.

The proposed Bareilly urban area has been divided into six planning districts each showing the sites of the centres of employment, general industries and occupations, playgrounds community facilities and residential areas within its limit. Each planning district with its own district centre, having facilities of retailing and other necessities, will act as a complementary unit to the whole city.

Proposed Bareilly urban area (10354 hectares) includes the area of Bareilly Municipal Board (2560 hectares) and 36,392 hectares of the area of under taken 198 villages. The Master Plan envisages the following pattern land use in the city.

TABLE 7.1 **Proposed Landuse of Bareilly for 1996.**

	Landuse category	Land in hectares	% of Total
1.	Residential	3932	39.0
2.	Commercial	391	3.5
3.	Administrative	263	2.5
4.	Industrial	2001	20.0
5.	Public and Semi Public facilities	2878	28.0
6.	Roads and Railways	890	8.0
		10,354	100.0

1. RESIDENTIAL AREA

The master plan has earmarked new areas for the development under residential land uses with a view to solving the housing problem of the city and beautifying the city. The new residential areas are meant for the migrants in the city and for an estimated population over a period of two and half decades. Due to paucity of land available, the plan suggests that larger bungalow-plots of the Civil Lines be subdivided into smaller ones to provide accommodation for the lower and middle class people. The plan aims to open the highly congested inner part of the old city, and suggests renewal programms for thinning out the congested inner zone.

The Plan reserves a total 3931 hectare of land for residential purposes. According to them this has been allocated in the following manner : 1041 hectares for low density (150-200 persons per hectare), 1461 hectares for medium density (200-300), 1445 hectares for high-medium density (300-400) and only 84 hectares for high density (400 & above).

COMMERCIAL AREAS

There is provision to lessen the pressure of the main markets of the city by separating the two functions, the retailing and the wholesale activities. Wholesale grain, bamboo, and vegetable markets are proposed to be shifted near Mental Hospital on Shahjahanpur Road. An area of 49 hectares has been ear-marked for this purpose. Retail vegetable markets of Kutubkhana is to be shifted near Saraikhan. City centre is proposed to be developed near Surkha village (N.W.) on a 125 hectare land while wholesale market is to be shifted near Pilibhit By-pass. There is a proposal of one district centre in each planning districts.

INDUSTRIAL AREA

The trend of industrial component of working force in total population shows that this proportion would increase from 28 per cent in 1961 to 35.5 per cent in 1996 and by that time Bareilly will emerge as an industrial city. The Master Plan believes that the present mills and factories will remain where they are and proposes to expand Fatehganj (west), C.B. Ganj and Izatnagar. New areas reserved for the location of industries for future are (i) Near Ramganga Bridge on Budaun Road (187 hectare), (ii) On Pilibhit Bye-pass road (79 hectares) and (iii) Near Shahmatganj Railway Station (28 hectares).

ADMINISTRATIVE AREA

At present government offices are mostly concentrated in Civil Lines. An area of 140 hectares near Central Jail on Nainital Road has been allocated in the Master Plan for the location of civic centres and offices.

COMMUNITY FACILITIES AND SERVICES

The plan proposes to provide better recreational, educational and health facilities for the citizen in future, based on socio-economic survey conducted by the department. To increased the present share of recreational land of 0.2 hectare per 1000 persons, a picnic spot is proposed in the north-west fringe near Teliapur village, one regional park in between Pilibhit Road and the Nakatia River and another near Rubber factory colony. This brings the proportion of recreational ground to .4 hectare.

UNIVERSITY AREA

Alongwith the provision of five more degree colleges located in different sectors of the city, sites for a University-cum-Research centre, an engineering college and a medical college have been earmarked between the Pilibhit Road and the river Nakatia on about 367 hectare.

Considering the present and future need of the people the plan has earmarked 31 hectares of land for the construction of **5 new hospitals** each with the capacity of 500 beds. Similarly, 49 hectare of land has been proposed for scio-cultural institutions near the city centre and the city park.

The water and sewer schemes have been revised to provide pure water for every citizen and to have adequate sewer and storm drainage facility in the city. For this purpose the surface as well as underground water resources, are to be tackled. The plan proposes three sewerage farms: (1) in the south of C.B. Ganj Railway station (2) in the south of Budaun bypass and (3) near Fatehganj.

TRAFFIC AND TRANSPORTATION

Based upon the general survey of volumetric and directional traffic at certain points of the roads, the Master Plan suggests redevelopments of major intersections. To insure free movement of traffic, five intersections namely, Kutubkhana-Barabazar, Novelty Talkies, Ayubkhan, Shahmatganj and Chaupala-have been proposed for re-development. Thirteen existing roads, which are major traffic arteries, have been proposed to be widened for relieving traffic congestion. Important new streets to be opened up in the regulated area are shown in the Master Plan (Fig. 7.2).

The proposed by-pass roads joining Budaun Road with Rampur Road and Shahjahanpur Road with Pilibhit Road are very important from the stand point of intra-city movement and daily business needs of the city. The Master Plan further suggests opening up of some radial roads, seven underpasses and five overhead bridges and also construction of some approach and ring roads.

An area of 8 hectares has been proposed on Rampur Road in front of Industrial Training Institute for bus terminus and its workshop. The existing roadways workshop on Shahjahanpur road has been recommended to be used as truck terminus.

The existing CB Ganj railway station has been proposed to be expanded while Shahmatganj railway station will be used both for the passengers and goodstraffic.

OTHER PROPOSALS

The existing sugar and other chemical factories located at Nekpur are proposed to be shifted to the proposed industrial area on Budaun Road. The existing slaughter houses and dumping grounds will be shifted beyond river Nakatia outside the future urbanisable limits.

MASTER PLAN : A CRITICAL REVIEW

The main object of the city planning is to enable every inhabitant of the city to enjoy full health of mind and body. A majority of the citizens of Bareilly are compelled to live in old delapidated houses completely lacking in essential amenities. In the old city these houses are so closely built up that fresh air and sunshine, so essential to the building of a sound physique, can hardly penetrate. The planners of the Master Plan themselves estimate that about 29 per cent of the city's population are living in slums which is an insult to the modern civilization. But no solid proposal has been made in the Master Plan for the renewal of the inner zone where a majority of slum dwellers reside. A number of residential colonies have been proposed in the plan for the fringe area without any detail regarding the accommodation of these people. It is likely that these colonies might be occupied by higher income group people.

The Master Plan of Bareilly is exclusively concerned with the physical construction of the city. It has not taken into consideration the basic factors which face the town at present, ie., employment of a high percentage of unemployed persons of the city and the fringe. The Master Plan must provide proper opportunities for the employment of the people by assessing the commercial and manufacturing requirements and potentialities of the city.

Further, the Master Plan has not given due consideration to the increasing gap between urban and rural set up of the area specially in the fringe. There is a tendency to grab agricultural land and push up land prices. It increases exploitation and conflict.

The next shortcoming in the Master Plan is about the newly suggested sites for industries. The plan proposes shifting of the industries from the inner zone to the southern part of the city just north of Ramganga Bridge. The proposed site suffers from two defects : firstly it is just by side of the residential area and secondly there is no scope for further extension of this industrial zone. It is advisable that this industrial zone may be shifted towards the east of the Budaun Road where enough land is available for further extension and it is separated from the residential area by road and railway tracks.

The major defect of the Master Plan appears to the author is that it incorporates a larger area for the improvement without any geographical consideration. The fringe which is a geographical unit should have been taken into consideration for the further development of the area. The author is of opinion that the planners have been overenthusiastic in their approach, which may not be a reality. Similarly the proposed construction of a number of ring roads and the location of different institutions suffer from same defects. Perhaps the planners have not taken into consideration the huge financial involvement that the city has to face for the implementation of the plan.

SCOPE OF RECONSTRUCTION

The main objective of the foregoing study and analysis has been to provide a detailed base for the scientific planning and improvement of the town and its fringe. Throughout the study a geographical perspective has been kept in view. Planning of a city needs not only the skill and assistance of engineers and architects but also the help of geographers.

After analysing the various aspects of Bareilly and its urban fringe brings us to make a few remarks regarding the possibilities of its planning and improvement. It is concluded that the city needs a comprehensive regional planning along with the fringe.

With the growth of population and increase in the complexity of function in the city, a centrifugal force has come into operation and the surplus population is likely to move in the fringe. The urban fringe area has inadequate sanitary facilities, medical facilities and other utility services due to the presence of low income group people in this belt and therefore unbalanced growth of the city and fringe takes place.

The unplanned development of the city and its fringe taken together have resulted in the continuous disturbances of the rural-urban relationship and widening the social and economic gap between the two. These are hindering integrated development of the region. A comprehensive development plan for the town, is highly desirable in which emphasis should have been laid not only on the growth of the city but also on the integration of both the city and the fringe, with a view to maintain ecological equilibrium. Only such a comprehensive approach can overcome the urban misery and the rural poverty.

With the limited scope of the present study it is not possible to discuss extensively various aspects of town and country planning. However, an attempt is being made here to broadly outline the main features of the development plan for Bareilly and its urban fringe.

The greatest difficulty facing the planners is the administrative division of the area, as the city is governed by the corporation while the development of the rural area is under separate authority. It is not possible for the town planners to give due importance to fringe development and hence the development in the fringe is rather slow and is not keeping pace with the city. Moreover, further development of the city is possible only in the fringe where regulatd and coherent development is highly desirable.

DEVELOPMENT OF THE CITY AND ITS FRINGE : FEW SUGGESTIONS

As a matter of fact planning for the fringe belt is actually urban planning of the city for the future, because a town usurps the fringe in due course. Therefore fringe planning is extremely important.

HOUSING

As discussed in the foregoing the city is faced with serious residential and housing problems. The inner zone consisting of 29 per cent slum dwellers needs urgent renewal. The process may be lengthy and irksome. The life of the houses should be fixed under certain regulation and demolition of old and delapidated houses will take after the expire of the life of the houses. No building activity should take place in the space left for. Such method in the course of town will automatically open the congested inner zone. The corporation will be able to plan the development of this area on scientific basis.

As the population of the town is growing at the high

rate the number of additional houses required for the growing population and the migrants will be very large. It is proposed that for these new comers as well as for those who can afford to shift outside, some new residential colonies may be developed in the fringe on neighbourhood pattern.

From geographical point of view taking into consideration the topography, accessibility etc. the author proposes two larger residential colonies to be developed in the fringe. First in the south-eastern part along Shahjahanpur road where new developments are already taking place. Another site is proposed on the area south of Rampur road near C.B. Ganj. The first colony will cater the housing needs of university staff, engineering college and commercial areas nearby while the second colony is meant to provide accommodation to industrial workers and other employees of the area.

BUSINESS AND SHOPPING CENTRES

The present business areas and centres have developed along the major thoroughfares and regional routes without leaving much space for parking and for loading and unloading of goods. As such the customers are put to great inconveniences. The author is of the view that it is not feasible to make any great alternation in the existing business structure of the town as it will involve the dislocation of the whole structure. However, the existing condition may be improved under a long term plan involving the widening of main business thorough-fares, provision of ample parking, loading and unloading space.

Keeping in view the increased business activity and needs of the city, provisions made by Master Plan for the extension and expansion of wholesale market and to develop a 'city centre' near surkha in North-West are being proposed in the same manner. But the planners have not paid much attention to local shopping centres, highly essential for the locality. However, the location of shopping centre in each planning district is also inevitable to lesson the burden of main business area of the city in future. It is suggested that the Civil Lines shopping centre near Railway Station be improved by allowing their expansion along the main routes which will be able to cater for the needs of the greater part of the sough-west block of the town. The main business area of Barabazar will, of course, meet the entire commercial needs of the whole northern and eastern part of the city.

In order to meet the business requirement of the fringe the existing market centres of C.B. Ganj, Izatnagar should be improved and new business centres should be developed at Pilibhit Road, Budaun Road and Shahjahanpur Road, and at the proposed residential colony outside the present municipal limit. About 75 to 100 shops and stalls should be erected within a radius of half kilometre. Further there must be provision for shops in each residential sector of 200 families to provide vegetables and grocery etc.. The proposed business centre of the city will also meet the urban needs of the neighbouring fringe villages.

INDUSTRIES

FUTURE SITES

The manufacturing and industrial zones should be separated from residential zones and be located at suitable areas in the fringe. At present most of the small scale and household industries are located in the built up area of the inner zone of the city where there is acute shortage of land and most of the industries, are being run in the residential houses of the owner and artisans. It may be added that industrial overcrowding in the city is not desirable but there does seem to any remedial alternative for the present. However, it is proposes that big industries should be developed in C.B. Ganj, Izatnagar and the satellite town Fatehganj West. The small scale consumer goods industries alongwith cottage industries should be developed in the fringe villages. It will also provide employment to the villagers to improve their economic conditions. In this regard two proposed industrial areas of Budaun and Pilibhit Roads are appropriate and they should be developed to produce the consumer items for daily use in the city (Fig. 7.3).

Further, the location of HR Sugar and Chemical industries at present in Nekpur is most uneconomic and detrimental to the interest of the local urban community. The shifting of these factories to the proposed industrial estate is needed. The present site thus left may be used for the manufacture of furniture and cane industries for which the city is well known.

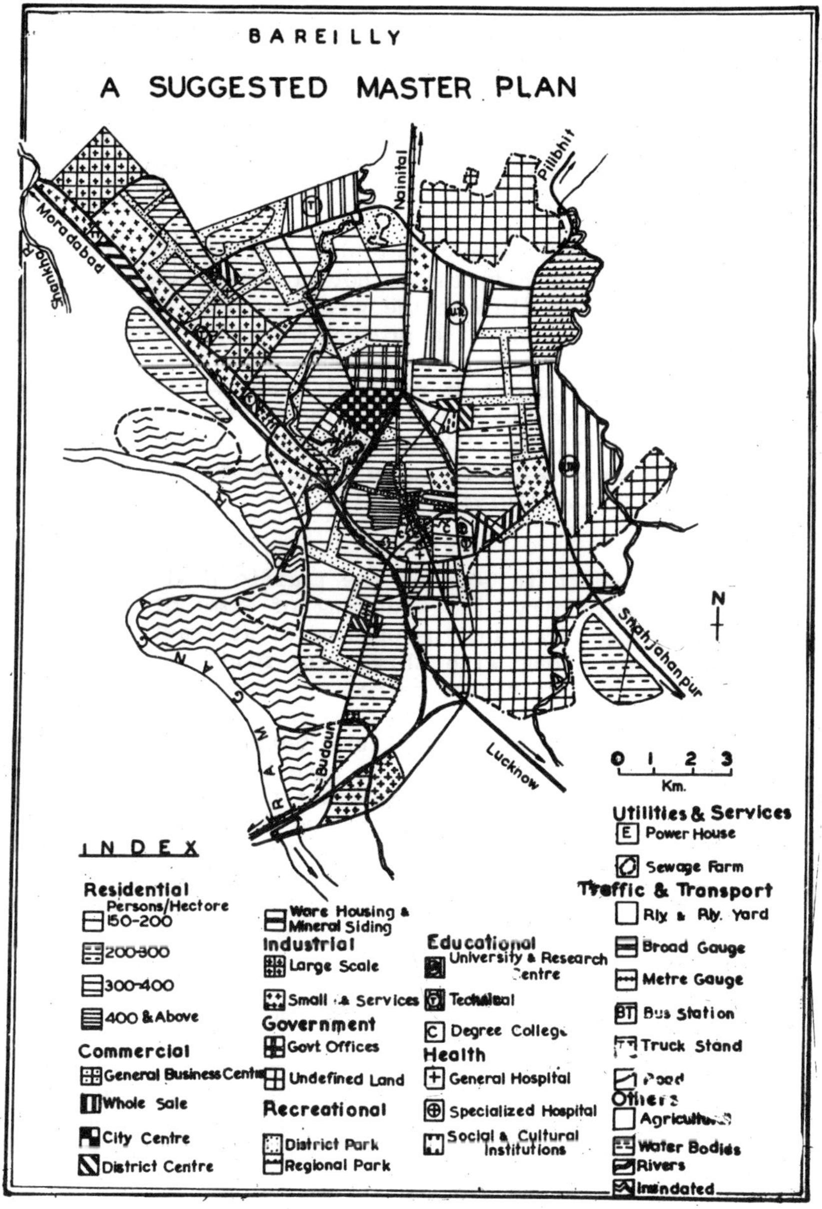

TRANSPORTATION AND CIRCULATION PATTERN

Provision for adequate transport facilities are the basic need of the city. The important roads of the city which need the widening and improvements are the Quilla-Shahmatganj road, Kutubkhana Koharapir road in north and Kalibari road in South. The Master Plan has rightly suggested about 13 roads to be improved to reduce the congestion.

In order to divert heavy vehicular traffic from the main thoroughfares of the city the author proposes a scheme of 3 ring roads passing through the western fringe of the city following, more or less, the present municipal boundary in that direction. A number of bypasses have also been suggested to link the important regional roads outside the main builtup area in order to facilitate the movement of outbound heavy vehicular traffic without entering into the city. The width of the roads proposed to be 30-40 metres so that they may accommodate the increased traffic even in future (Fig. 7.3).

Thus, the shift in some of the traffic producing functions of the main city, the widening of some of the main business thoroughfares and the opening of at least two north south bypasses along with three ring roads may solve the traffic problems to a higher degree.

In order to provide better links between the city and its fringe a number of link roads have been proposed which will almost interlink all the important places of the fringe with the city. The existing unmetalled roads of the fringe should be metalled and improved. Village roads which generally follow the chak roads have been proposed to link the villages with the main regional roads so that villagers could easily commute to the city centre, place of work and market etc.

PUBLIC UTILITY SERVICES AND COMMUNITY FACILITIES

As discussed in the foregoing, the public utility services and community facilities provided to the citizens of the city are not adequate. An adequate water supply, sewerage and sanitation facilities, health and electricity are the need of the hour. So far recreational facilities are concerned, it is proposed that in the flood affected south western part of the fringe an artificial lake should be constructed. This lake will be attractive for boating. The fishery industry may be developed here to supply fish to markets in Bareilly. It may be highly attractive to the tourists.

THE EDUCATIONAL AREA

The Master Plan rightly suggests the north-eastern part for the educational centres. The University area has been suggested to cope with the demand for higher education. A site for Medical College in the Western outer fringe has also be proposed in this area.

LANDUSE PLANNING

The landuse planning involves two separate types planning ; one for the city and another for the fringe. Mention has already been made regarding the planning for the built up area, neighbourhood, open spaces and playgrounds etc. for the city. For the development of the fringe it is proposed that original pattern of landuse may be maintained as far as possible. The fringe area which is highly rural and where land is quite fertile may be a source of green vegetables, dairy products and fresh fruits etc.

In the south and south east the whole area is fit for horticulture. Although in the south of Shahjahanpur road a lot of land is given to grow vegetables, it is proposed that area south-east of Cantonment may be intensively used for commercial agriculture. Thus the market gardening must find sufficient place in the outer fringe replacing the general agriculture of cereals only.

If all the measures proposed for the development of the city and its fringe are implemented properly, the city alongwith its fringe will generate forces of economic growth, occupational diversities, social mobility, in short, a new way of life.

REFERENCES

Alam, S.M. and W. kHAN (1972) **Metropolitan Hyderabad and its Region. A Strategy for Development**, Asia Pub. House, Bombay.

Fiery, W.I. (1946) Ecological considerations in Planning for Urban Fringes, **Amer. Social Rev.** Vol. II, pp. 411.

Kumar, P. (1980) **Agricultural Changes in Urban Fringe**, Rajesh Pub. New Delhi, pp. 187-190.

Singh, U. (1973) Cities of the Ganga Plain, Their Problems

and Planning, in R.L. Singh (Ed.) **Urban Geography in Developing Countries**, pp. 343-350.

Strachan, A. (1974) The Planning Framework for Modern Urban Growth, in Johnson J.H. (Ed.) **Suburban Growth**, pp. 53-75.

Urban Land-Problems and Policies, **Housing and Town and Country Planning Bulletin-7, United Nations**, New York.

APPENDIX I

Bareilly Urban Agglomeration : Population Figure

Wards	Area in Hectare	Population 1961	Density Km^2	Population 1971	Density Km^2	Variation in Density	Literacy percent	Sex Ratio F/1000 M
1	44.0	10944	24.4	23330	52.1	113.2	20.5	844
2	60.0	14621	243.7	17897	298.3	22.4	30.00	891
3	28.8	19342	671.6	16344	507.5	-15.5	65.00	903
4	43.2	16933	392.0	15544	359.8	-8.2	45.00	871
5	463.0	17332	37.4	21094	45.6	21.7	46.00	829
6	40.8	8968	219.8	15013	368.0	67.4	53.00	780
7	440.0	18249	41.5	14252	32.4	21.9	33.00	840
8	31.2	13359	428.2	16222	520.0	21.4	01.00	892
9	88.8	15970	178.7	18048	203.2	13.7	54.00	890
10	36.0	13358	315.5	17470	485.3	53.8	44.00	876
11	213.6	18215	85.3	19441	91.0	6.7	35.00	859
12	55.2	13691	248.0	22268	403.4	62.6	23.00	888
13	156.0	15274	97.9	19299	123.7	26.4	21.5	876
14	55.2	18078	327.5	21006	380.5	16.2	31.00	879
15	67.2	23970	356.7	18203	270.9	23.6	20.00	867
16	218.4	18205	83.4	20822	95.3	14.4	47.00	832
Cantt.	1712.0	13205	7.7	18270	10.7	38.4	60.00	807
N. Rly.	26.0	2564	98.6	3508	135.0	36.8	50.00	580
Izat N.	300.0 (119 in 1961)	2650	22.3	8080	27.0	204.9	60.00	776

APPENDIX II

Bareilly: Occupational Structure, by Wards: 1971
(percent of total workers)

Wards	Agriculture and allied	Industries H.H.	Industries Manf.	Construction	Commerce	Transport	Other Services
1	13.6	3	23	5.5	12	23	20
2	1.0	10	27	6.0	23	12	20
3	1.0	5	21	2.0	27	8	35
4	1.0	3	22	8.0	19	17	28
5	3.0	6	9	5.0	15	14	48
6	16.0	1	16	3.0	27	22	33
7	8.0	6	21	5.0	18	19	24
8	2	1	18	1.0	31	14	38
9	0.5	2	25	6.0	18	14	35
10	1.0	13	26	1.0	22	13	22
11	2.0	3	24	0.0	23	25	21
12	2.0	14	34	3.0	18	13	17
13	13.4	9	29	8.0	9	10	18
14	1.0	4	20	0.0	29	19	26
15	5.0	7	25	3.0	14	21	24
16	5.0	2	9	0.0	13	32	35
NRC	–	–	–	–	–	93	7
Cantt.	1	2	3	–	3	4	85
Izat.	–	–	41	2	1	45	11

NRC = Northern Railway Colony
Izat = Izatnagar Railway Settlement.

APPENDIX III

VILLAGES IN THE URBAN FRINGE OF BAREILLY - 1971

Sl. No	Village Code No.	Name of Village	Area Km^2	Population	N.F.W. %
1	192	Mehgawan	628	961	13.8
2	197	Behti Den Jogir	263	436	6.0
3	198	Itauna Sukhdeopur	337	958	16.0
4	199	Sanaiya Dhahsingh	306	946	3.0
5	200	Sithaura	375	1088	32.0
6	201	Benipur Chaudhari	277	407	5.5
7	203	Sarai Talfi Must	414	586	15.0
8	206	Bhagotipur	201	93	5.0
9	207	Rutha (Must)	109	879	8.0
10	210	Sanian	387	1610	25.0
11	211	Chandpur Jogian	134	833	35.0
12	212	Chandpur gogan	268	758	63.0
13	214	Jogither	337	1159	24.0
14	218	Hyderabad	682	1600	43.0
15	220	Mathurapur	511	1146	14.0
16	221	Tilliapur	546	3068	33.0
17	222	Bandia	473	1761	15.0
18	408	Bangarnagar Sundarasi	317	476	7.0
19	409	Sarai Rani Mewakuwar	674	1285	14.0
20	410	Jauharpur	462	1415	62.0
21	411-412	C.B. Ganj Khalilpur	443	7542	96.0
22	413	Moheshpur Attaria	586	1226	34.0
23	415	Budhaulia	177	1641	19.0
24	416	Sanaura	233	353	12.0
25	417	Medapur	149	190	15.0
26	418	Govindpur	207	1226	3.0
27	419	Mohalau	219	484	45.0
28	420	Shikarpur Chaudhary	166	524	74.0
29	421	Faridpur	195	2034	90.0
30	422	Partapur Chaudhari	88	1448	13.9
31	423	Raipur Chaudhari	282	1454	-
32	424	Mahlaxmipur	82	331	5.1
33	425	Central Jail	-	2628	4
34	426	Math Kavol Lainpur	85	503	Central Jail
35	427	Saidpur Hakins	679	1804	6
36	428	Surkha Chhawani	600	516	2.6
37	429	Udaipur Khas	1412	1595	0.8
38	432	Kanja das pur	269	714	29
39	433	Nagaria Parixit	158	886	2.6
40	435	Girdharipur	172	364	2.2
41	436	Nagaria Kalan	772	1176	2.2
42	437	Bhura	435	1487	1.5

43	438	Chanwar	480	681	3.4
44	439-40	Pir Bahora	631	4450	1.4
45	430	Behamman Nagla	1636	4335	7.1
46	431	Pratapur Jiwansahai	160	617	2.6
47	441	Khajuria Zulfiquar	304	482	3.9
48	444	Dhaunera	419	478	1.6
49	445	Sherpur	226	136	0.9
50	446	Tulapur	171	298	0.5
51	374	Kumrah	438	753	1.6
52	377	Rajpur Maufi	248	607	3.1
53	378	Mundia Ahmadnagar	948	1436	2.4
54	391	Bilwa	546	595	1.5
55	392	Karimpur Chaudhary	471	1054	1
56	393	Ata Kayasthan	395	966	2.4
57	536	Dohara	330	834	2.4
58	538	Newada Jogian	625	1504	4.6
59	539	Jagatpur Lala Begam	396	300	29
60	540	Newada Sheikhan	243	363	24
61	541	Haru Nangla	619	1297	29
62	544	Bharataul	238	737	33
63	545	Saidpur Khajuria	579	2557	56
64	546-47	P.A.C. + Mohanpur			100
65	548	Naryawal	661	4784	31
66	549	Padarathpur	298	2787	6
67	557	Thiriya Nizabat Khan	906	8146	40
68	558	Chanetha	302	1301	21
69	560	Kandharpur	345	1692	45
70	564	Kareli	865	3063	40
71	565	Abhaipur Khand	60	272	42
72	559	Chanethi	147	944	60
73	566	Kargaina	612	1782	67
74	567	Nekpur	1108	187	75
75	568	Maheshpur Thakuran	627	984	89
76	576	Arguri	471	966	23.6
77	582	Pargawan	344	1002	42

NFW = Non Farm workers as percentage of total workers
Sl. No. = Serial number on base map 2.7.

BIBLIOGRAPHY

BOOKS

Alam, S.M., **Hyderabad-Secunderabad, A Study in Urban Geography**, Allied Publishers, Bombay, 1965.

Alam. S.M. and Khan, **Metropolitan Hyderabad and Its Region**, Asia Publishing House, 1972.

Berry, B.L. and Horton F.E. **Geographic Perspectives on Urban Systems**, Englewood Cliffs, 1970.

Carter, H., **The Study of Urban Geography**, Arnold, London, 1972.

Carter, H., **Cities in the Suburbs**, Toronto, 1962.

Coleman's Alice : **The Planning Challenge of the Ottawa Area**, Geogl. Paper No. 42, 1969.

Coppock, J.T. et.al., **Greater London**, Faber & Faber, London, 1964.

Deshpande, C.D. et.al., **Impact of a Metropolitan City on the Surrounding Region: A study of south Kolaba, Maharashtra**, Concept, New Delhi, 1980.

Dobriner, W.M.. **Class in Suburbia**, Englewood, Cliffs, N.J. 1963.

Dube, K.K. **Use and Misuse of Land in KAVAL Towns**, N.G.S.I. Varanasi, 1976.

Garnier, J.B. and Chabat, G., **Urban Geography**, Longmans, London, 1967.

Gibbs, J.P. **Urban Research Methods**, Van Nostard, New York, 1966.

Gopi, K.N. **Process of Urban Fringe Development A Model**, Concept, New Delhi, 1978.

Gottman, Jean, and R.A. Harper (Ed) **Metropolis on the Move: Geographers look at Urban Sprawl.** John Wiley, New York, 1967.

Gottman, J. **Megapolis: The Urbanized North-Eastern Seaboard of the U. States**, The Twentieth Century Fund, New York, 1961.

Hall, P., **The world cities**, London, 1966.

Johnson, J.H. **Urban Geography, An Introductory Analysis**, Pargamon Press, London, 1967.

Johnson, J.H. (Ed.) **Suburban Growth: Geographical Processes at the Edge of the Western City**, John Wiley, London, 1974.

Lal, H., **Jansankhya Bhoogol** Vasundhara Prakashan, 1986.

Kumar, Pramila: **Agricultural Changes in Urban Fringe**, Rajesh Publications, New Delhi, 1980.

Mandal, R.B. and V.N.P. Sinha (Ed.) **Recent Trends and concepts in Geography, Vol. III**, Concept, New Delhi, 1980.

Martin, W.T. **The Rural Urban Fringe: A Study in Adjustment to Residential Location**, Uni. Orezon Press, Eugene,1953.

Mayer, H.M. and C.F. Kohn, (Ed.) **Readings in Urban Geography**, Univ. Chicago Press, 1967.

Misra, R.P., **Habitat Asia - Issues and Responses**, Concept, New Delhi, 1979.

Murphy, R.E. **The American City - An Urban Geography**, Mc Graw Hill, New York, 1966,1980.

Nangia, Sudesh: **Delhi Metropolitan Region : A Study in Settlement Geography**, K.B. Publication, New Delhi, 1976.

Noble, A.G. and A.K. Dutt (Ed.) **Indian Urbanization and Planning, Vehicles of Modernization**, Tata Mc Graw Hill, New Delhi, 1977.

Paul, R.E. **Urbs in Rure - The Metropolitan Fringe in Hertfordshire**, London School of E & P.S. Geogr. Paper No. 2. 1965.

Rao M.S.A. **Urbanization and Social Changes, A Study of a rural community on a Suburban Fringe**, New Delhi, 1970.

Rao Prakasa, V.L.S. (Ed.) **Readings in Planning and Development**, Golden Jubilee Volume, IGS Madras, 1976.

Rao Prakasa, V.L.S., **Urbanization in India. Spatial Dimensions**, Concept, New Delhi, 1983.

Schimid, A.A. **Converting Land from Rural to Urban Uses**, Washington, 1967.

Schnore, L., **The Urban Scene**, New York, 1965.

Singh, H.H. **Kaupur: A Study in Urban Geography**, Indrasani Devi, Pub. Varanasi, 1972.

Singh, R.L. **Banaras, A Study in Urban Geography**, Nand Kishore, Varanasi, 1955.

Singh, R.L. (Ed.) **India: A Regional Geography**, N.G.S.I. Varanasi, 1971.

__ **Rural Settlements in Mansoon Asia**, NGSI, 1972.

__ **Urban Geography in Developing Countries**, NGSI, Varanasi, 1973.

Singh, U. **Allahabad, A Study in Urban Geography**, B.H.U.

Press, Varanasi, 1966.
__ **Nagariya Bhoogol**. U.P. Hindi Granth Academy, Lucknow, 1974.
Sinha, M.M.P. **The Impact of Urbanization on Land use in the Rural Urban Fringe: A case study of Patna.** Concept, New Delhi, 1980.
Sovani, N.V., **Urbanization and Urban India**, Asia Pub. Bombay, 1965.
Spectorsky, A.C., **The Exurbanities**, New York, 1955.
Sunderam, K.V., **Urban and Regional Planning in India**, Vikas, New Delhi, 1977.
Thomas, D. **London's Green Belt**, London, 1970.
Turner, R. (Ed.) **India's Urban Future**, Univ. California Press, Berkeley, 1960.
Verma, Pramila, **Competition for Land Between City and Farm with special Reference to Edinburg**, Rajkamal, Delhi, 1966.
Wadhva, Kiran, **Urban Fringe Land Markets, An Economic Analysis**, Concept, New Delhi, 1983.
Wissink, G.A. **American Cities in Perspective with special Reference to the Development of their Fringe Areas**, Assen, 1962.
Yadav, C.S. (Ed.) **Perspectives in Urban Geography: Vol 9. : Rural Urban Fringe**; Concept, New Delhi, 1987.

ARTICLES IN JOURNALS

Alpake, F. (1942) "Landuse control in the urban Fringe of Portland Oregon", **Jl. of Land and Public Utility Economics** Vol. 18, pp. 463-78.
Andrews, R.B. (1942) "Elements in the Urban Fringe Pattern", **Jl. of Land and Public Utility Economics**, Vol. 18, pp. 169-83.
Aschman, F. (1949) Dead Land, **Land Economics**, Vol. 25, pp. 240-45.
Bagchi, K. (1956) "The Howrah Conurbation A Study in urban sprawl", **Geogl. Rev. of India**, Vol. 28, pp. 16-31.
Balk, H.W. (1945) "Rurbanization of Worcester's Environs", **Eco. Geog.** Vol. 21, pp. 104-116.
Beegle, J.A. (1947), "Characteristics of Michigan's Fringe Populations, **Rural Sociology**, Vol. 12, pp. 254-63.
Blizzard, S.W. and W.F. Anderson (1952) "Problems in Rural Urban Fringe research-Conceptualization and Delineation", **Pennsylvania, Agri. Exp. Stn. Progress Report**, 89, p. 11.

Bore Gowda, P. (1981) "Dynamics of the Rural Urban Fringe: A case study of Bangalore" **Unpublished Ph.D. Thesis**, Univ. Mysore 1981.

Brookfield, H.C. (1952), "The Geographical Study of Urban sprawl of western Cities", **Indian Geogl. Jl.** Memorial Vol. pp. 101-05.

Brush, J.E. (1968) "Spatial Patterns of Population in Indian Cities", **Geogl. Rev.** Vol. 58, pp. 362-391.

Chatterjee, A.B. (1965), "Hinterland of Symbolic City: A case study" **Geogl. Rev. of India**, Vol. 24, pp.55-71.

Colby, C.C. (1933) "Centrifugal and Centripetal Forces in Urban Geography", **Annals of Assn. of Amn. Geogrs.** Vol. 23, pp. 1-20.

Conzen, M.R.G. (1960) "Alnwick Northumber land: A study in Town Plan Analysis", **Trans. Inst. Br. Geogr.** Vol. 27, p. 58.

Davis, I (1953) "Urban Farming: A Study of Agriculture of city of Birmingham", **Geog.** pp. 298-303.

Dayal, P. and B. Thakur (1976) "Commercial Ribbon in Patna, Spatial Growth and Functional Structure, **National Geogl. Jl. of India**, Vol. 22, pp.

Fesanmairer, D.R. and Others (1979) The Spatial structure of the Rural urban Fringe: A multivariate Approach, **the Canadian Geog.** Vol. 23, pp. 255-65.

Fiery, W.I. (1946), Ecological considerations in Planning for urban Fringes, "**Amer. Social Rev.** Vol. 11, pp. 111-23.

Giggs, J. (1970), Fringe Expansion and Suburbanization Around Nottingham, **En. Midland Geogs.** Vol. 5, p. 9-17.

Golledge, R.G. (1960) Sydney's Metropolitan Fringe: A study in urban Rural Relations, **Australian Geog.** Vol. 7, pp. 243-55.

Harvey, R.O. and W.A.B. Clark (1965) "The Nature and Economics of Urban Sprawl, **Land Eco.** Vol. 41, p. 72.

Hayes, C.R. (1957) "Suburban Residential Land Values along the C B & Rail Road, **Land Eco.** Vol. 33, pp.177-81.

Hudson, J. (1973) "Density and pattern in Suburban fringes" **Annls. Assn. Amr. Geogr.** Vol. 63, pp.28-39.

Jadhav, R.S. and G.S. Kulkarni (1967) Landuse planning in the Rural urban Fringe of Poona, '**National Geogl. Jl. India**, Vol. 13, pp.158-67.

Johnson, R.J. (1966), "The Population Characteristics of the Urban Fringe A Review and Example", **Australian and New-zeland Jl. of Socl.** Vol. 22, pp.19-33.

Kurtz, R.A. and J.B. Eicher (1958) Fringe and Suburbs A confusion of concept, **Social Forces**, Vol. 38, pp.32-37.

Kurtz, R.A. and J. Smith (1961) "Social life in the Rural Urban Fringe, **Rural Sociology**, Vol. 26, pp.24-28.

Lal, H. (1972) "Gradients of Urban Influence on the Rural Settlement concentrations with special Reference to Bareilly, "In R.L. Singh (Ed.) **Rural Settlements in Monsoon Asia,** NGSI, pp. 264-272.

__ (1973) "Urban Fringe: An Analysis of concept' **Uttar Bharat Bhoogol Patrika,** Vol. 9, pp. 64-72.

__ (1980) "Urban Fringe, Concepts and Delimitation, in R.B. Mandal et.al. (Ed.) **Recent Trends and concepts in Geography,** Vol. III, pp. 121-141.

__ (1980) "Spatial Distribution of Population in City and Fringe, **Earth Science Digest,** Vol. I, pp. 79-88.

__ (1983) Urban Fringe of a North Indian Town: A case study of Bareilly, **Market Studies, The Indian Jl. of Marketing Geography,** Vol. 19, pp.40-48.

Morril, R.L. (1965) Expansion of the urban Fringe, A Simulation Experiment, **Pap. Reg. Sci. Ass.** Vol. 15, pp.185-199.

Mukherjee, D. (1963) The concept of Fringe and its Delimitation: A case of Orland, Florida, U.S.A., **Geogl. Rev. India,** Vol. 25, pp.45-55.

Masser, F.I. & D.C. Stroud (1956) The Metropolitan Village, **Town Planning Rev.** Vol. 36, pp. 111-124.

Martin, W.T. (1953) The Rural Urban Fringe: A Study of Adjustment of Residence Location, **Univ. Oregon studies in Sociology,** Vol. 7, p. 3.

Myers R.B. and I.A. Beegle (1947) Delineation and Analysis of the Rural-Urban Fringe; **Applied Anthropology,** Vol. 6, pp. 14-22.

Martin, R.C. (1973) Spatial Distribution of Population, Cities and Suburbs, **Jl. Reg. Sci.** Vol. 13, pp. 269-278.

Mc Kain. W.C. and R.G. Burnight (1953) The Sociological Significance of the rural urban Fringe from the Rural Point of view, **Rural Sociology,** Vol. 18, pp. 109-16.

Pryor, R.J. (1964) Urban Fringe Residence: Motivation and Stratification in Melbourne, **Aust. Geogr.** Vol. 11, pp. 148-56.

__ (1968) The Sampling Frame for the Rural Urban Fringe, **The Profnl.. Geogr.** Vol. 20, pp. 251-261.

__ (1968) Defining the Rural Urban Fringe" **Social Forces,** Vol. 47, pp. 201-215.

__ (1968) Accessibility in Melbourne Fringe' **Research Paper in Geography,** No. 15.

__ (1969) "Delineating outer Suburban and the urban Fringe" **Geografiska Annaler,** Vol. 51, pp. 33-38.

Queen, S.A. and D.B. Carpenter (1953), The Sociological Significance of the Rural Urban Fringe from the urban point of view, **Rural Sociology,** Vol. 18, pp. 101-107.

Rikkinen, K. (1972) "Boundary Changes in a Rural-Urban

Fringe Areas", **Acta Geographica**, Vol. 26, pp. 25-26.
Rodehaver, M.W. (1947) Fringe Settlement A Two Direction Movement, **Rural Sociology,** Vol. 12, pp. 47-57.
Schnore, L.F. and V.K. Klaff (1972) Suburbanization in the Sixtees. A preliminary analysis" **Land Eco.** Vol. 48, pp. 23-33.
Singh, L.R. (1964) "Changing Landuse pattern in the Urban Fringe of Allahabad: Umarpur Niwar A Case Study", **Trans. of the Indian Council of Geogrs.** No. 38, pp. 32-45.
Singh, U. (1966), "Urban Fringes in KAVAL Towns" in R.L. Singh (Ed.) **Applied Geography,** NGSI, Vns. PP. 41-48.
Smith, D.L. (1966) "Market Gardening at Adelaids Urban Fringe" **Eco. Geog.** Vol. 42, pp. 9-13.
Srivastava, B. and R. Ramchandran (1974) The Rural Urban Fringe, **The Indian Geogl, Jl.** Vol. 49, pp. 1-9.
Wehrwein, G.S. (1944) The Rural Urban Fringe, **'Eco. Geog.'** Vol. 18, pp. 217-228.
Whitehand, J.W.R. (1967) Fringe Belt: A Neglected Aspect of Urban Geography, **I.B.U.** No. 41, 223-34.
__ (1972) Urban rent theory, time series and Morphogenesis, **Area,** Vol. 4, pp. 213-33.
Wolf, R.I. (1965) Nucleation on the Rural Urban Fringe, **Ekistics,** Vol. 20, pp. 228-31.

GOVERNMENT PUBLICATIONS

Census of India 1981, Series-1, India provisional population, Totals : Rural Urban Distribution, Delhi.
District Census Handbook of Bareilly, 1951, 1961, 1971, Allahabad.
District Census Handbook, Bareilly Distt. Town and Village Directory, 1971.
District Gazetteers-Bareilly, Allahabad, 1968.
General Population Tables pt II-A, **Census of India,** 1971.
Master Plan for Bareilly (Draft 1971-1996) Bareilly Survey Division. Town and Country Planning Department.

Index